PENGUIN BOOKS

RAINFOREST

Jenny Diski was born in 1947 in London, where she lives and works. She is also the author of *Nothing Natural*, which received universal acclaim, *Like Mother*, *Then Again* and *Happily Ever After*.

Jenny Diski

RAINFOREST

PENGUIN BOOKS

PENGUIN BOOKS

Published by the Penguin Group
Penguin Books Ltd, 27 Wrights Lane, London W8 5TZ, England
Penguin Books USA Inc., 375 Hudson Street, New York, New York 10014, USA
Penguin Books Australia Ltd, Ringwood, Victoria, Australia
Penguin Books Canada Ltd, 10 Alcorn Avenue, Toronto, Ontario, Canada M4V 3B2
Penguin Books (NZ) Ltd, 182–190 Wairau Road, Auckland 10, New Zealand

Penguin Books Ltd, Registered Offices: Harmondsworth, Middlesex, England

First published by Methuen London Ltd 1987
Published in Penguin Books 1988
3 5 7 9 10 8 6 4 2

Printed in England by Clays Ltd, St Ives plc
Filmset in Plantin

This book is for Chloe Diski
with all my love

In a sense chaos is missing information. It is what human beings observe when they don't have access to the information needed to see the underlying order.

Dr Joseph Ford
Physicist at Georgia Institute of Technology

Perhaps randomness is not merely an adequate description for complex causes that we cannot specify. Perhaps the world really works this way, and many events are uncaused in any conventional sense of the word. Perhaps our gut feeling that it cannot be so reflects only our hopes and prejudices, our desperate striving to make sense of a complex and confusing world, and not the ways of nature.

Stephen Jay Gould
Hen's Teeth and Horse's Toes
Reflections on Natural History

One

I clean houses for a living. That is, I earn my money that way. After I left the hospital I found that making other people's houses tidy satisfied me, and once the word got round, I had enough clients to keep me occupied for as much of the week as I wanted. I have a regular schedule. I freelance. I go from one house to the next according to the day of the week, dusting, polishing and straightening, replacing things in their owners' order for them to come home to.

There were other options. I could have gone back to what I did before. Not to the forest, of course, but to an academic life. It would have been possible to return to teaching and reviewing the work of other researchers. I thought that was what I would do and mulled it over in the hospital, discussed the way back in with my doctor, who seemed to think it feasible, provided I left the field work to others. I, in any case, had no desire to return to the forest; it was enough, more than enough, that the forest came to me so frequently in my dreams.

What I like about the work is the detail and planning involved.

There are a dozen different ways one can set about cleaning a house. It can be seen as a series of levels: the floors, then the freestanding furniture, and finally the walls – pictures, shelving and so on. Or it can be carved into discrete spaces; individual rooms to be dealt with in rotation, one by one. Alternatively, each floor of the house can be designated a separate level, so that one begins at the bottom and works one's way up, or vice versa.

Even when the general approach is clear there remain decisions to be made about timing. Do you go through the whole house each session maintaining a general level of cleanliness and order, or do you designate particular tasks to each session so that, for example, all the floors can be thoroughly cleaned one week, and all the furniture polished the next? Each house requires its own decision; there are different needs that become obvious on the first visit and I find that if I walk through a house in the right frame of mind – calm, open, observant – the best approach comes to me.

Today, being Tuesday, I was at the Willing house. My favourite because of the order inherent in the place. There are really no decisions to be made about it, it needs only to be returned to its original state, only to be maintained.

The house is modern, built only a few years ago by an architect much admired for his uncluttered designs. It is functional but elegant, an ideal place for a professional couple with a certain style and good taste who have no plans for children.

I let myself in with my key at ten o'clock. By then Max and Julia have breakfasted and left for work – he designs machines, computer hardware, she teaches drawing at an art school. When I arrive there are small signs of occupation: the breakfast things are neatly stacked in the sink, the pillows on the bed dented and the duvet pushed back to reveal the creased white bottom sheet. Sometimes, if there was company the night before, there are cigarette stubs in the ashtrays. The Willings themselves do not smoke.

I like to begin by getting these details out of the way. I wash the two small plates, the two breakfast cups and saucers, the knives for buttering the toast, and put them all away. Then I return the butter dish to the fridge and the marmalade jar to the cupboard. I unscrew and wash each section of the Italian percolater, drying them carefully before putting it back together and replacing it on the shelf where the tea- and coffee-making equipment are kept. Then I go to the bedroom: plump up the pillows, smooth the bottom sheet and shake out the duvet, all white.

This morning the ashtrays were unused, but there were some things on the glass coffee table, apart from the two Netsuke figures and the small glass bowl that holds dried rose petals: a new novel that Julia had been reading, and several copies of *New Scientist*. I put the magazines into a pile and took them into Max's study; the book I left where it was, but slipped the leather bookmark that lay beside it between the open pages and closed it.

I begin in the living room.

The walls and woodwork are white. A rich, deep white that comes from many coats of good-quality paint, each new coat sinking deep into the last, reflecting and drawing out the whiteness beneath until finally the whiteness *is* the wall and not mere pigment spread on to a surface. A single painting breaks the solid whiteness of the walls. It is made up of blocks of pale colour, each outlined strongly with a darker line, as if it were a jigsaw, arranged but not yet fitted together, suggesting a still life, flowers, a book, perhaps, on a table, but only suggested, not defined. Below this painting is a low white sofa, and on the light woodblock floor in front of it lies a single, richly coloured kelim, glowing with forms that suggest nature but are in fact, when you really look, geometry. In front of that is the low glass table and facing the sofa, two chairs of pale leather, sharply square and outlined in chrome.

This room pleases me immensely, not that it's a room I would choose to live in, I wouldn't want it for my own, but it's so complete, so entirely itself, that I have only to remove disturbances to bring it back to what it's supposed to be.

I begin with the floor, brushing the kelim carefully, then sweeping the wood with a soft brush before I wax it. Next comes the glass; I polish the table above and below, clean the inside of the windows and the glass that protects the painting. Then I dust, wiping the leather and chrome of the chairs, and finally stroking clean the tiny Netsuke figures: the bent old man with his cane and the fat self-satisfied duck, its head nuzzled back preening its feathers. There is no question that when I have finished the room is itself again, revealed but not created. There is such satisfaction in making it simply *right*, so that when the Willings return home they notice nothing out of the ordinary, nothing jars, things are simply as they are supposed to be.

*

There are some places that I won't take on, that don't conform to the rules that I suppose I have set for myself, and the result is that quite accidently I have achieved a rarity value; it's as if I go with a certain style of living. Just as it is meaningful to have fabric from this shop or furniture from that, so to have Mo Singleton cleaning your house means something among a particular group of people. It would have been clever of me had it been deliberate because I can now ask for more than the going rate, but in fact my acceptance or refusal to clean a house is about my own requirements.

It is important to me that the house doesn't remind me of anywhere I have lived, that there is nothing I can personally identify with – I want only to make order, no, remake it, not to feel anything about it. And for much the same reason it is essential that the people who live in the house are out when I am there. I won't clean the house of anyone who works at home or on shifts. I need to know that when I put my key into the lock the place is empty, so that when I shut the door behind me and stand for a moment in the entrance, no one will call out a greeting. I like to hear the sound of my footsteps in the hall, put down my bag and coat and be able to feel the absence of people. It's a temporary absence, of course, the remnants of the morning or the night before testify to that, people were here and will be again, but now, right now, there is no one here and I can go through the place and put it all right.

The other condition, although I don't state it, is that there are no children. I don't dislike children but, for them, *things* are important not the spaces the things inhabit. It's obvious that they do have a sense of order, but it's order of their own devising, not, like adult order, tied into the needs of their physical surroundings. I respect that but I can't cope with it. I can't dust around what I perceive as mess however much I know that it has a meaning for the child. So no children.

I clean one house a day for four days of the week and earn enough to live on. On Wednesdays I see Dr Taylor at the hospital for an hour at nine thirty and then I'm free. The pattern of life suits me, I like the schedule and the fact that it's of my own choosing. Life is organized and busy. At weekends and on my free day, I read and walk. Sometimes I see people; my mother, of course, and Nick. I'm not bored or uncertain about how to spend my time. I feel sometimes, when I'm sitting quietly, that I've been very fortunate, things have worked out surprisingly well for me. Sometimes, as I mentioned, my sleep is disturbed, but Dr Taylor says it's to be expected and probably time will take care of that. I'm aware that to some people my life will seem rather barren, but I can only answer them by saying that to me their lives are frenzied and frantic and no more purposeful than my own. In any case, it's a matter of emphasis. If I describe my work as the centre of my life, it's because I take a pride in it. *How* I work is what is important to me and it gives me a great deal of pleasure to know that I haven't lost that. *What* I do matters much less, and I've discovered that it's possible to approach cleaning houses with the same care, the same rigour, as I have used for other tasks, previous employment. I am still who I am, the continuity is there.

I had another dream last night; a forest dream.

I was back in the forest working on my project, checking over the information I had gathered that day, collating it. I sat in my tent in the clearing bent over the figures and felt the sweat running in droplets down my back and from my armpits. My scalp itched with the heat and damp. It was quite real, just like it was, until I looked up from my notebooks suddenly aware that something was wrong, and saw that the tent had disappeared. No tent, no desk, nothing; I was alone standing in the tiny clearing surrounded by the edges of the forest. All around me tree trunks soared a hundred, a hundred and fifty feet into the air, massive vertical columns disappearing into the dense, deep green, light-defying gloom overhead. I stood in the perpetual greenish twilight and felt fear rise and spread, creeping within me like the lianas that were everywhere, twisted and snaked around themselves and anything in their way.

I heard the sounds of the forest, the normal sounds of monkeys screeching, birds hooting and crying. The noise of movement, sudden and swift in the canopy, branches cracking, leaves rustling; the long, rasping sound of things creeping, sliding, scuttling below on the forest floor, and always the incessant, mechanical sawing of the cicadas and the wailing frogs. Noises I had lived with for months, but now I stood alone, and the clearing seemed to shrink as the sound expanded.

The forest closed in on me, and suddenly the noises weren't the ordinary or extraordinary sounds of the forest, alive and separate, but speech. The howling and screeching and rustling, and the rhythm of the cicadas were talking to me, but in no language I could understand. The forest intended me to listen to its gibberish, required me to hear it and receive its incomprehensible message. I knew each separate sound was meant for me, had a meaning, but the sounds confused and reverberated on each other until there was nothing but mad noise, and I began to scream against it, to be released from it.

There was now no more than an arm's width between myself and the trees surrounding me, as they encroached further without seeming to move at all. I panicked in the dismal twilight and heard my scream mingle with the chattering of the forest, and I fell on my knees, crying out, 'I can't hear you. I don't understand. Please leave me alone.'

And, as ever, I woke then, soaked in the twisted sheets of my bed from the sweating and the sobbing, and, as ever, it took me a moment to understand in the darkness that my room was my room and not the forest trees, retreating from my fear and confusion.

Nick came round this evening. We ate sardines on toast and drank a can of lager each. We were both tired from the day; I had cleaned the Willings' house and Nick had had his usual day in the library making his discoveries and connections and juxtapositions for The Book.

'Are you busy? Can I come in?' he asked anxiously as I opened the door. I was pleased to see him and smiled into his wide, worried eyes to reassure him.

'Hello. Come in, I was just going to open a tin of something – sardines or baked beans – which?'

He came in and sat down at the table, more anxiety playing around his eyes and creasing his brow as he tried to make a decision.

'Oh – sardines? Yes, sardines. Is that all right? Or would you prefer baked beans?'

'No, sardines are fine. OK.'

Nick sat and watched me cut bread and open the tin. He wore his usual ancient tweed jacket, bought from an Oxfam shop a decade ago, threadbare where it isn't patched, old Levis, and the crew-neck Shetland sweater I gave him for his birthday. Nick is quite unable to cope with his appearance, he doesn't notice things, couldn't care less about what he wears, but worries because he knows that clothes and how people look matter to others. We often discuss the possibility of his buying a new jacket or a pair of trousers. He asks my advice very seriously: where should he go, what colours, shape; and I try, although clothes don't interest me greatly either. But we both know that he'll never get round to doing anything about it. I've offered to go shopping with him and he seems pleased, but somehow a date is never set. He is actually perfectly happy with what he has, and when the jacket finally falls apart or the jeans go to holes, he will then drop into a local jumble sale and find replacements. Nick is certainly unkempt in his person, but his face is fine and classical. He is quite beautiful; with his blond curly hair and blazing blue eyes he might have stepped out of a Renaissance painting. The long aquiline nose and high flattened cheekbones give him an heroic look. But his mouth is troublesome, thin-lipped and straight, a narrow gash that surprises you with its hardness, and makes you think again before investing him with the gentleness the rest of his face suggests. But the gentleness is there, it was what first attracted me about him. That and his ability to sit quietly with me when I needed it. We met in the hospital and he came and sat with me in the dayroom, quiet and kind. We would talk sometimes; sometimes he just held my hand.

This evening, as usual, he told me how The Book was getting on, of his researches that day in the library.

'It's there, Mo, it's all there,' he said, animated as ever by his topic. 'I'm on the right track. It'll take time of course to uncover it all, weave all the threads together, but every day a new piece falls into place. If I can only find a way of translating the maths into language . . . But I will, it will come to me. Do you know, there's an equation – a mathematical equation – now for *chaos*? They're getting so close, it's only the language that defeats them.'

Nick's excitement is contagious, but also disturbing, since its source is madness; a controlled madness, but I've seen what happens when he loses that control, and it frightens me for him. For months now he has been poring over scientific papers and journals, reading up on the latest work in quantum physics, information theory, biochemistry, ecology, philosophy – all the varied attempts to define the nature of existence. He moves with ease between establishment science and metaphysics, taking in any degree of speculation on the way. Everything is potential grist to the mill, it is all possible information, because he knows that eventually, under some unlikely and probably unrespectable stone, he will find the key. The missing piece that will make everything else fit together. He isn't unique in this search, others have tried, but Nick is certain that he will finally understand, and find a way of explaining to a waiting and dying world the meaning of it all.

I don't know. As I say, I fear for him, but I find his stories of 'what's going on' out there in the scientific world interesting. He uses me to practise translating maths to language.

'What do you mean "an equation for chaos"? If you can formulate chaos, it isn't chaos any more – surely?'

'Yes, yes, exactly,' his eyes light up, 'it means that chaos is no longer beyond our comprehension, it's part of a process, not the end, not outside human understanding. Our science couldn't deal with unpredictability, it was outside its scope, but now it can be brought in. We don't have to stop, defeated by our hopeless imagination. I think we've found a way to use the structure of the brain to go beyond the limitations of that structure. Do you see?'

'No. It sounds more like poetry or philosophy, not a practical scientific explanation. Chaos is still chaos, something that can't be thought.'

'But it can *now*. We have the formula for it so we can include it in our thought. We have the symbols for it. It's obviously an essential part of the system. *The System*,' he emphasized. 'Now we have the maths for it we can go further.'

What worries me is that Nick will achieve madness before synthesis. The line between is so finely drawn and he has slipped into it before, it is the easiest route to a complete truth that would satisfy him. I can feel it sometimes in myself when we talk, although of course I am much more careful than he is. I think that maths was invented to avoid madness; it's what the scientists use to stop themselves going crazy – mostly it works. If you can represent infinity by the letter 'n' then you can deal with it. You don't have to think about infinity itself, it's just another variable to be considered, not a meaningful concept that is emptied of meaning because we aren't equipped to think about it. 'n' means infinity, infinity means nothing. Poets and philosophers go crazy, mathematicians stay sane by limiting the dreadful things they have to think about. But Nick wants to take those safe formulae and translate them back into meaning. He is like a child, he has no idea of the danger. For me there's joy in learning that there's a formula for chaos, I don't want to have it turned back into language and process. The point is that there isn't enough language to explain what we really fear, that is what the arithmetic is for. I know chaos but the words I have for it won't do, nor the thoughts. I will not allow chaos into my mind any more, and if someone has made it into an abstract symbol then I applaud them for making it unnecessary to use words, or to tear one's mind to pieces in the effort to make sense of what is not sensible.

None of this, of course, can be said to Nick. He wouldn't understand. So I listen and encourage, so far as I am able.

Later we went to bed. Everything this evening was as usual. We undressed on opposite sides of the bed, Nick dropping his clothes on the floor. I folded mine over the back of the wooden chair. Then we turned down the spread together and slipped between the white sheets. Nick put his arm under my head and asked softly, 'All right?' I said, 'Yes,' and turned my head to kiss him gently on the cheek. He put his hand over my breast and squeezed it for a second, then kissed me carefully on the mouth. His hand moved down my body and came to rest between my legs, doing nothing but being in what he supposed to be the right place. I closed my eyes and remembered another hand that had played on my body. The memory of that hand made me ready for Nick as he pushed into me and moved up and down in his stolid rhythm, until after a few minutes he climaxed, grunting, 'Mo . . . Mo . . .' Then as usual I moved underneath him, pressing against his pubic bone until I had relieved myself, and my small, restrained cries told him that I had finished too.

'I'm sorry. Was it too soon? Are you all right?' he whispered, touching my cheek before he rolled over to his side of the bed.

'I'm fine. Don't worry, it's all right.'

The fact is that Nick isn't very interested in sex. Although we make love like this once or twice a week, it isn't an important part of our friendship. But it makes him feel better, and does no harm. I don't mind, only sometimes as I lie awake next to him my body remembers and I touch myself until I come shuddering in silent sobs of disappointment, pressing my mouth against the pillow to suppress the sound, angry at myself for such indulgence.

Tomorrow after Nick has left I'll see Dr Taylor, then I'll come home and clean up the flat. In the afternoon I'll go for a long walk in the park; it's Wednesday, my free day.

Two

Then.

Back a year. Before it seemed that anything had happened. When life was quite straightforward and could be expected to proceed according to plan, and when the forest still only whispered in Mo's ear, so quietly and in such oblique tones, that she heard nothing.

It was October, the beginning of the academic year. Mo had spent the summer vacation setting up her project in Borneo. Her research grant had gone through and she was to spend the following spring and summer at a research station in the heart of primary rainforest, studying its ecosystem for her doctoral thesis.

She had been lecturing in the Life Sciences department of the university for two years. The thesis was simply a part of the process; a continuation of a career that hardly needed planning, an academic progress that, barring accidents, just happened. The choice of what she wanted to do in life having been made (and barely made, it had been so obvious) at school, everything else followed unsurprisingly.

Still, sitting on the plane on the way to Sarawak at the beginning of the three-month summer vacation, she was quietly gratified with the way things were going. She had talked to people and written letters and had a clear idea of the bureaucratic hurdles she needed to jump to get to the research station.

It began almost as soon as the plane touched down in Sarawak. First in the teeming cities and monumental government buildings, talking to people, arranging transport and obtaining initial permits. Then on, to progressively smaller centres where the official stamps got more impressive as the population and the size of the municipal offices decreased; until, finally, civilization was represented by a lone, uniformed official sitting behind a rickety metal desk in a wooden hut, who signed and sealed the last permit with a Napoleonic flourish and warned the pale, serious young woman in front of him against the dangers she faced.

'The forest bad place. Rotten. Steamy. Make people ill. You take care. Mosquitos. Snakes. And bad dreams. You take care, young girl.' He stabbed his finger at the desk as he spoke, making it shudder with each of the evils he enumerated.

Mo smiled her thanks at him. 'Yes, I will be careful. I'm well prepared.'

But he shook his head doubtfully. She didn't know. So young, a woman, far from home. He knew she didn't know, but what could he do other than warn?

A guide was found to take Mo into the forest proper, and the place that was to be her base for the next three months.

She packed her book and papers, tins of food, survival equipment, and set off finally with Leloh, a local villager, upriver in the longboat that served as taxi for the comings and goings of the field workers. The research station was several miles away in a clearing by the river that snaked its way through the dense forest, and was most easily reached by boat.

They made the slow, winding journey through a dramatic limestone gorge, the river banks lined with crammed, competing trees and foliage – rambutans, wild figs, sago palm – growing with greedy gusto by the water's edge in the rare, unobstructed sunlight that the gash of the river permitted. She sat in the longboat searching the passing river bank with binoculars and was rewarded frequently with sightings of creatures that stopped in their tracks, poised between curiosity and fear, to watch the floating tree trunk and its noisy, wrong-smelling inhabitants. Troops of leaf monkeys stopped and shrieked at one another to take care; swifts swooped and flashed their brilliant markings in the sun. A sambur deer appeared out of the dense foliage to drink at the water's edge, and froze at the strangeness that was passing by, its russet coat quivering with attention in readiness, should its stillness not render it invisible, to bolt back into the concealing forest. A warbler's cry pierced the buzzing air, issuing a warning and asserting its territorial rights. Up ahead, a small family of otters made haste to get away from the oncoming disturbance, recognizable only by their sleek shapes cutting through the water. Beside them, for a moment or two, a crocodile glided and then turned towards the bank, more intent on basking in the sunlight than investigating the unnatural sound that sputtered from the ancient outboard motor.

At each sighting Mo would turn round to Leloh who, being an old hand at ferrying these scientists back and forth, told her the Be-rowan name for the creatures she had seen. It was a form of com-munication. Mo would repeat the word and smile a thank you. Sometimes Leloh would point to a tree whose branches lolled down into the water and volunteer its name and mime whether its fruits were delicious or dangerous to eat. Or he would point out a passing butterfly, a birdwing, brilliantly black, green and red, or a grey and white wood nymph which Mo had missed because her binoculars were for seeing what was in the distance, not what passed within inches of her head. She complained in sign language and grimaces of the clouds of mosquitos that accompanied every moment of their journey, and Leloh nodded vigorously, laughed and waved his arms wildly around his head in pantomimed agreement and aggravation.

He had come to understand, gradually, about these visitors from far-away cities, how they had another way of looking at things. They wanted names and descriptions; to look at things, but not to touch or use. He had names for things, of course, but along with the word came pictures and memories of the part the thing played in his life and the life of his people. There were many words for liana, de-pending on its qualities of thickness or suppleness, the way each might be used, some for lashing timbers together to make sturdy long houses, some for delicate nets that would provide food from river and forest. Things were known by names, but inside his head by their qualities. The outsiders wrote names of things in books and gave Leloh another way of thinking about them. Like their cameras and tape recorders, they used words to carry bits of the forest away to strange and unimaginable places (though he had seen photographs of great stone buildings and landscapes where all signs of natural growth had disappeared) without the need for having the things themselves. He found this interesting, and supposed that the hunters and providers in those far places had other ways of doing things. It was necessary, he knew, to have a sense of the world one lived in and used, a feeling about it that was more than the names one spoke aloud to tell others that it was there. Early on, when the research station was first erected, he had expressed his friendship for the foreigners by bringing them what he thought they wanted. After a difficult conversation, all signs and drawings, he realized that his new friends were asking about a particular kind of creature – they called it a silvered leaf monkey – and he had spent most of the next day in the forest with his bow, returning to the camp triumphant with a still-warm furry grey corpse slung over his shoulder. But they had looked uncomfortable and talked in worried tones to one another, with much waving of arms, and finally one of them who spoke a little Berowan explained that it was bad to kill the creatures of the forest, and that they had wanted only to find the monkey so that they might look at it. They spoke very gently to him, as if he were a child, about the forest dying and the need to look after the things in it. It didn't seem to him that the forest was dying, there was plenty for everyone, but he respected their beliefs and kept his hunting skills for himself and his family, and thereafter offered only names of things and directions for finding them.

Now Leloh helped Mo unload the longboat and stack the boxes on the jetty, then smiling and waving and promising to see her soon he left.

The research station was a rectangular timber structure built along the lines of a local village long house, raised on stilts some six feet off the ground against the frequently flooding river and marauding rats. It was set about twenty yards back from the river and the tiny jetty that served it, in a small clearing. So small that the zinc-roofed building seemed to crouch fearfully beneath the massed trees that soared above it, surrounding it on three sides. It seemed to be digging itself in against the pressure of the forest that almost perceptibly crushed forward. It was only a matter of time, Mo thought, as she stood with her bags and boxes beside her, before the forest would overcome the tentative man-made thing that huddled in the clearing and push it off the bank for the river to carry away, all resistance finally useless.

Mo chided herself for thinking such anthropomorphic nonsense, picked up her rucksack and headed for the wooden steps that led up to the entrance.

It was an internationally funded centre that scientists and monied amateurs came to for periods according to the vagaries of funding and fashion. It was used as a base camp for the various sub-camps where the detailed field work went on, and provided technical support – equipment, radio and a central collection point for supplies – as well as a necessary rest from the intensity of days or weeks in the interior of the forest. The researchers, each intent on studying their particular speciality, were all glad of the opportunity to relax in the evening, or after an extended period at one of the remote sub-camps, and share beer and conversation. Often men from the local village, some five miles away, would drop in to join the company of the strangers in their midst and to offer their services collecting specimens or guiding. It was a convivial place and Mo was immediately made welcome by the two current residents who came out shouting greetings and helped her bring in her things.

She stayed for a time at the station with a biologist who studied frogs, and another specializing in the feeding pattern of a particular species of termite, while she worked out her supply requirements and explored the surrounding forest, instantly dense beyond the clearing. In the evenings she drank beer and listened to the advice the old hands offered, making notes and asking questions. During the day she made trips to Sub-Camp 3 in order to familiarize herself with the area, seeing it as a tailor might a bolt of cloth. She wanted a piece, cut from the whole, on which to chalk her pattern; for in order to study the interaction of so complex an environment it is necessary to divide it into segments, to place over a small patch of forest a grid of squares, and to note exactly, day by day, everything that occurs within its boundaries. When, after months, the information is collected and transferred to graphs and subjected to statistical analysis, it is possible to begin to get a picture of the whole life of the forest in a way that is simply not possible to an observer who merely stands and looks and makes his own private interpretation of what he happens to see.

She went into the forest every day with her notebook and made maps and plans and sketches. When she found the areas she was looking for, she paced out what were to be their boundaries, and noted down all the main features within the designated perimeters. She worked, as she always worked, carefully and conscientiously, knowing that this preparatory task was vital if her research was to succeed.

The forest was good for Mo. She lived in it as a scientist, an observer with a clear intention, practising on it. It was her material, her source of study. That it was also her temporary home, her environment, was accidental, a function of the size of the thing she was observing and of the fact that her interest was in the living balance, the thriving system. To find out how that worked it was necessary to be in the field; to measure and collect, to count and name. Later the results of her observations could be transferred to a laboratory or computer and analysed at leisure. In the meantime she had to live with the forest in order to find out how the forest lived. But not as part of it. She knew herself to be outside the order she intended to find. That was, of course, the only possible position for the observer. She had to be on the spot to collect the data that was touched by her only at the moment of recording. Her eyes and then her pen would note; sometimes her hands would physically remove the information from its surroundings for classifying and measuring. *Then*, at that time, she knew, she had created a disturbance in the natural behaviour of what she studied, but it was not an idea she took very seriously, or even thought about very much. She left that to the philosophers and went about her work as a practical scientist, content that, for all realistic purposes, she studied the life of a virgin forest that was quite unaltered by her alien presence in it. Indeed, her guarantee of its being unaffected by her was precisely her degree of alienation. Things as different in kind as rainforests and human beings were not altered by one another, providing the human beings were present in small enough numbers and kept their imaginations for more creative leisure activities. Naturally people changed their environments, used them, altered them beyond recognition; but not individual scientists, merely observing, at worst carrying off tiny fragments to study. And certainly environments affected people if people let them. Nothing could be easier than to transform accidental features of light and shadow, shapes thrown up by natural growth, sounds created by wind and the obstacles in its path, into the atmospheric stuff of poetry and emotion-rousing, meaningful symbols of human happiness and sorrow. But it was not necessary. The trained observer had to clear away all the old images from storybooks and films, and *see* things for what they were. Be fascinated by shadow, but fascinated to know exactly why and how the light rays had been blocked. Be moved by birdsong, but move in the direction of understanding the natural history of that particular bird and the reason for its cries.

But Mo was not completely immune to the experience of being in a tropical rainforest. She did notice the stunning heat and the desperate humidity. She did feel the discomfort of clothes that were drenched with sweat within seconds of putting them on. She did have a sense of being enclosed by the looming canopy of branches and leaves that blocked out the sun, and used the word 'gloom' in her notebook to describe the resulting darkness, and the strange, dismal, dank green mist that hung in the air. But she knew also that all those things were physical facts that followed from the nature of the environment she was in. It was to be expected. As were the ants that carpeted the ground and trees, and bit everything, including her; and the spiders, some so large they might, from a distance, be mistaken for small mammals. This was rainforest: an untouched, physical world that teemed with the life that created the environment, which in turn allowed that life to teem. It was her job to observe the forest and analyse its parts; to understand the system. She was not there to react to discomfort or fear, or that odd sense of foreboding that came over her as she entered the shadows from the bright light of the clearing. At least, not react so much that it prevented her from doing her job effectively.

Nor was the rainforest completely immune to the experience of Mo.

To say that the forest was conscious of Mo would be inaccurate, since consciousness was not the nature of the forest. Nor awareness. One might say that the forest included Mo in itself, as its many components took her existence in. Or, at any rate, her behaviour. The subtle but definite alteration that Mo made by her presence made her a part of its existence. The compound eye of the forest received her in the multiplicity of ways that added up to sight, or knowledge.

The breaking of a shaft of light as she passed through it. The shifted angle of a leaf as she brushed it aside. The sound of her pencil scratching across paper, reverberating slightly but persistently through the atmosphere. The minute change in carbon dioxide levels as she breathed. The re-routing of a column of soldier ants, made necessary by her footfall. The sudden interruption of play of an infant macaque as its mother grabbed it and fled from the alien sound and smell. All these things, that *were* the forest, were altered and alerted to another aspect of their environment: *there*, and therefore constituent.

The fact that Mo was new was not relevant, since time belongs to thought, and thought was not the mode of the rainforest. Things lived and died and decayed; but their elements remained, even if those elements were washed away by the rain into streams, then rivers, and then carried up and away into other atmospheres, other places. Still, everything belonged; and having thoughtlessly contributed, continued forever to be of the forest, no matter if its elements were physically dispersed. Everything remained, part of the continual present. Known.

So Mo, being there, was of the forest, part of it. Her awareness or consent were not required, any more than the consent of a molecule of H_2O, or a pitcher plant, was needed to make them a part of the multiplicity of the forest. Forever.

When her three months were up, Mo had finished her preparations and made her arrangements. She retraced her route, back down the river, through villages, towns and cities, to London, in good time to begin the new term. The preliminary visit had gone well and she was quite confident about next year's expedition. The forest would be a fascinating object of study, and she looked forward happily to the spring when she could begin the project.

Three

Meanwhile Mo sat in her office at college, a few days into the new term, having just finished working out the first-year tutorial timetable. She had laid her notebook aside and was beginning to read an article in the new edition of *Nature*, when the door flew open and Liam stamped, groaning, into the room.

'Tiresome, tiresome children,' he announced, his eyelids heavy with disdain. 'Where are the new thoughts, the originality, the insights? This university is no more than a finishing school for the slow-witted. All the really bright kids are out robbing old ladies and vandalizing phone boxes.' He banged the door shut and poured himself a mug of coffee from the electric percolator. 'Mo, are you listening?'

'Not really, Liam, I've heard it before. I'm reading an article on incest avoidance in primates.' She laid the magazine down and glanced up at him. 'What happened?'

'Oh, nothing much.' He slumped into the armchair beside her desk and crossed his legs comfortably. 'Just tedium – and tits. There seem to be a lot of tits about lately. Must be the unseasonal weather. Those girls do not dress properly. It's very hard to conduct a serious seminar on the lineage mode of production when no one has anything to say and a dozen stiff little nipples are pointing contemptuously at you.'

'You're just a dirty old man, Liam,' Mo said vaguely.

'And an unsuccessful one, my dear. Now you never expose your breasts, do you? They're always sensibly concealed under your very practical shirts and sweaters. Are they beautiful, your tits? I suspect that beneath your shapeless jeans and workaday shirts lies a body of surpassing loveliness. Just tell me.'

'I'll do.' Mo went back to her journal. 'You're upset by the heat.'

It was one of those miraculous London autumns that made winter seem improbable.

'No, I'm upset by youth. Specifically, female youth. Sitting there, exposing themselves, and pretending that all anyone has on their mind is the neo-Marxist analysis of pre-capitalist societies. Those that bother to pretend they have anything on their mind at all. They think they're irresistible and, of course, they are. All that fresh young flesh flaunting itself, tight, firm, oozing sex. But what they don't realize is that they're interchangeable. Desirable meat. Ripe and ready for the taking. There's no telling them apart. Some bits are better than others, of course. One's tits, another's arse, but ask me to put a name to any of them, or to distinguish them by the quality of their thought, and I couldn't. I'm depressed.'

Mo put the magazine down again. 'You sound it. How are Sophie and the kids?'

'Fine. All fine. The new baby sleeps like a baby and Sophie is already bustling wonderfully about working on her thesis.' Liam smiled with pleasure as he spoke. 'It's only my soul that's unhappy. I'm a spiritually unhappy man, Mo.'

'I know. Never mind, imagine how awful it would be to be spiritually unhappy *and* have a bad marriage.'

'Why doesn't that comfort me, I wonder? Why are you so sensible, Mo, so young and so sensible? I wonder if you aren't a prig?'

'Probably,' Mo agreed.'That would make two of us. But I don't fight it.'

Liam grunted and blinked hard, the result of a tic that punctuated his face throughout his waking hours rather than surprise at Mo's assessment of him. He frowned into his coffee so that his thick, sandy-coloured eyebrows formed a hairy ledge over his small, always humorous, ever-blinking grey eyes, almost the only part of his face that was visible under the dense tangled beard that covered him from cheekbone to neck.

Mo got up and poured herself some coffee.

Liam had been a senior lecturer in social anthropology for ten years when Mo arrived, a bright, promising biology graduate, two years before. He had taken her under his wing once it was established that she was neither shocked nor titillated by his cynicism and despair. He had spent his youth wandering and searching. As the second son of a landed Anglo-Irish family, he would not inherit and so had to find a place for himself in the world. Two centuries ago that would have meant the army or the church, but in the disarray of the early sixties when Liam left university, it took on a more precise meaning. Travelling to strange lands and exploring other cultures. Liam, being essentially conservative, justified his wandering by dropping English Literature and becoming an anthropologist. But at the back of it was religion. His High Anglican upbringing left him with an unsatisfied need for God, and in Asia and the Middle East he had sat at the feet of a variety of gurus. ('The real thing, the ones who had the truth and didn't care if you took it or left it; not these clever, westernized executive gurus who produce truth as if it were a McDonald's hamburger.') At one point he converted to Islam in order, he told himself, to investigate the Sufi sects, always justifying his God-search as anthropological. But his background was too strong; he returned home empty, atheist, cynical and, as ever, with a terrible, unfulfilled religious hunger.

'It simply didn't work,' he told Mo. 'I realized that eastern wisdom is for the East. I loved it and wanted it terribly, but it was not *my* culture. So I came home.'

His role in the department was Clown; not to be taken seriously by the other members of staff who, for the most part, were neo-Marxist theorists of the very latest kind. *Marxians* they called themselves, and regarded Liam's theoretical agnosticism as treacherous and weak-minded. While they fought battles, published papers re-analysing the nature of simple societies, denounced colleagues as Vulgar Marxists, re-made anthropology with models of base/superstructure and relations of production, Liam snorted and told the first-year undergraduates, 'You'll hear a lot in the next three years about economic bases and ideology, and modes of production, and jolly good stuff it all is too. Very useful way of looking at things, or one very useful way. But try not to forget, dear children, about people. It's very unfashionable to read ethnography at the moment, even more unfashionable to go out into the field and study other cultures; but do try and read the odd ethnography while you're here. Malinowski and Evans-Pritchard may be old-fashioned functionalists but you might find some of the things they had to say of interest. Not, of course,' he would add with a prolonged blink, 'that I expect any of you will take the slightest notice of what I say.'

For the most part the students looked at Liam's dishevelled, whiskered face and his shapeless old cord jacket and twill trousers, and saw his discomforting, unapologetic tic, and decided that being grown-up meant being on the other side. In any case, they were much too young to take being called 'dear children' lying down.

So Liam was as disregarded by the undergraduates as he was by his colleagues. A condition he loved, being the romantic he was, and he gained much pleasure from the irritation and dismissive glances of the young Turks of the department. Since Mo was a physical rather than a social anthropologist, she did not have to engage in the battle. No one had yet come up with a neo-Marxian interpretation of the eco-system. But Liam did manage an occasional dig at liberal-conservationist-do-gooders, and had given her a badge one birthday that said 'GAY WHALES AGAINST RACISM'. Mo had pinned it up happily on the noticeboard in her office.

Liam emerged from his gloom to look at Mo as she stood sipping coffee.

'You haven't answered my question. Why are you so sensible?'

Mo shrugged. She had hoped to avoid another of these conversations. 'I've always been sensible. I'm tidy and sensible. I don't like disorder. It isn't necessary. That's why I'm an ecologist, I suppose. I like to look at the world and find patterns. There are always patterns to be found. How else can one understand things?'

'But what about emotions, Mo? How do they fit in? Messy old emotions.'

'They're no more messy than anything else. Emotional behaviour can be as well understood as physical.'

'Not, surely, when it's your own emotional behaviour?'

'Why not? People who are confused about their emotional life enjoy their confusion. Most of the drama that goes on in people's lives is no more mysterious than anything else. I'd say that the interactions that go on in the average back garden are more complex than people's feelings. It can all be understood if there's a will to understand.'

'So no mystery?' Liam raised his bushy eyebrows in doubt.

'Not unless you want mystery.'

'Have you ever been in a situation you couldn't cope with?'

'No.'

'Oh Mo . . .' Liam murmured, disappointed, and blinked fiercely.

She began to find this conversation tiresome.

'I like my work, Liam, and I have friends. I don't need to make life into a grand secret. It's quite interesting enough trying to understand the way the natural world interacts. There are lots of things we still don't know about. I don't have to invent problems that aren't there to keep me involved.'

'All right.' He raised his hands in defeat. 'As long as you don't dis-invent problems that are there in order to stay sensible.'

'Well, I daresay time will tell.' Mo smiled amiably and returned to the journal. These discussions were a regular part of their friendship. Liam entertained himself with mystery and if he couldn't find any, concluded that there was the greatest mystery of all.

Liam watched her as she read and thought what a curious girl she was. Judging her from any visible angle one had to take her at her word. There was the mystery – it seemed everything was there to be seen. There was the problem – the mystery was that there was no deep mystery. Her clothes were practical and sensible: comfortable, loose jeans; chunky knitted sweaters; men's shirts; sometimes a skirt of the same family as the jeans. Ordinary, with no eye to a current trend for a particular shape or colour. The bulk of her wardrobe had probably stayed the same for the past fifteen years, things thrown out – sent to Oxfam, rather – only when they had started to wear, then replaced.

He took in her dark, almost black hair, which fell dead straight, parted at the centre, to a couple of inches below her shoulder. Lovely, rich-textured hair actually and, when you looked, an interesting face. If you looked carefully, intentionally. The long, narrow eyes behind the severe glasses were quite dark and surrounded by thick, unmascaraed lashes. The straight, sculpted nose. A real nose that gave character, and now he looked, an excellent mouth. Wide and almost sensual in the framework of her narrow face.

Why, then, was she so plain? She was a woman in her early thirties whom one would not glance at twice in the street. Something seemed to negate all the real interest that resided in the parts of her face. There was something boring about her looks that stopped you from noticing her physically, except with a special effort. Quite tall and slim; a good body, obviously; and nothing wrong, a good deal right, about her features. But it all added up to plain, dull, unattractive. Nice, but not interesting. Another woman with the same face would be desirable, but Liam could not work out why or how. Nothing to do with make-up or clothes – not really. But a quality in Mo that toned down everything until it became overall nothing. He liked Mo, but had never felt the slightest stirring of desire for her, beyond the desire to tease her a little. And yet, the thing was, that there was a quality about her that did not fit his dull assessment. Without that quality, whatever it was, he could have pigeonholed her neatly. She would be an older version of the students. Not the ones with the rampant breasts, but the others, the girls and boys who had studied diligently at school, gained good passes at A level, and continued to work industriously at university. No sparkle, but the work got done, what had to be understood was understood well enough and passed on in examinations. They had read only what it was necessary to read and as a result knew very little about life, and nothing, it seemed, had ever happened to them in their varying degrees of secure, suburban existence. No disturbances. Liam listened to their comments in his seminars and nodded his bored agreement as he heard that week's set reading efficiently paraphrased, while his real interest was grabbed by the odd one or two who perhaps had not done the reading, but had once read something that seemed relevant now, or who had *been* somewhere, or to whom something had happened in their eighteen years or so.

Mo could have been one of the first sort. He could imagine her an undergraduate, worthy, unimaginative and entirely unmemorable.

Except.

Liam was irritated at not being able to put his finger on what it was about Mo that made him sense there was something else – more or different. Her *sensibleness* just was not quite true and made him wonder (and only afterwards realize that he was wondering) where the mess was in her life. What dreams and nightmares did she have? Yet the wondering had no basis, not actually. There was not the slightest indication that there was anything more to her than what she showed and what she said was there.

'You intrigue me, little one,' Liam said.

Mo looked up severely. 'That's because you can't stand not to be intrigued, Liam. I'm interested in the ecology of rainforests. And I like teaching. I'm very happy with what I am and what I do, thank you.'

Liam lifted himself out of the armchair and made for the door. As he opened it he turned back thoughtfully: 'I'd still like to know if you have beautiful tits.'

'Go away and do some work, for God's sake,' Mo laughed as Liam looked especially lugubrious and left the room.

Mo's first-year lecture was about to begin, so she gathered her notes together from the drawer of the filing cabinet marked 'First Year'.

Her room was a model of efficiency. Another drawer of the cabinet was headed 'Xeroxes' and these were filed and cross-referenced under author and subject for ease of access. The shelves that lined the walls were filled with books, again ordered by subject and author, although books borrowed from the library had a separate section to themselves. Over her desk the pinboard was covered with postcards from friends and students, timetables, and small messages to herself, all carefully dated – 'for attention by . . .'

Mo shuffled her papers together and left the room. The lecture hall was in the same building down a couple of flights of stairs.

She was precisely on time, as were half the students. The rest arrived in small groups as she organized her papers on the lecture stand. When they were all settled, notebooks out, pens uncapped, she looked up smiling. This was to be the first in a term's course on Human Ecology and, since it was compulsory for all first-year social science students, the room was packed. Forty or more young men and women waited expectantly for her to start. There was, as Liam had said, nothing exceptional about them. They were a mass of faces, although during the term, after a few seminars and some essays had come in, she would begin to differentiate between them.

'Good morning,' she began. A few of the young women smiled a greeting, the rest waited. 'I want to start by giving you an overall picture of the work we will do in this course. Human Ecology is about the relationship between the human species and its physical and biotic environment. There are an immense variety of ecological strategies that exist in different human groups using different habitats, and the aim of this course is to look at the main environmental factors that influence man, to consider the biological constraints, and the adaptability that makes even the most inhospitable environments home for some group or other. We will deal with the following topics: the limits of human biological response to climatic extremes of heat, cold and altitude; the basic human nutritional needs; and the natural history of man's diseases caused by pathogenic organisms, and in particular their dependence on the way man has modified his own environment. Then we will consider the effects of these things on fertility, mortality and the resulting demographic trends in past and present human populations. Finally, we will look at man's impact on his own environment in habitat modification, pollution and over-exploitation. You don't have to write that down – it's all on the hand-out I am about to distribute.'

Mo was known throughout the department for the clarity of her lectures, and the students appreciated that. You never had to wait for the end of the lecture to know what the subject was, as with some of them. She began, always, by writing the main topics on the blackboard and kept to her scheme, although she did not read, but merely referred to her notes for the details. They were not exciting, there was none of the dash and wit with which some of the lecturers regaled their students. She did not ever attempt to entertain, or amuse, or prove how clever she was. Liam was the one for that. He would lace his lectures, the content of which interested him not at all at undergraduate level, with obscure quotes and sexual innuendo, entirely for his own amusement since the students almost never got the reference and usually missed or were embarrassed by the innuendo. But there was a flow and panache about them, added to strangely by his facial tic, that put some energy in the room. Mo's students took notes dutifully and with ease, since all the main points were either on the hand-out provided at the beginning of the course or written up on the board as the lecture proceeded. They got down all the relevant information, but found none of it exciting. She did, however, have the highest exam results in the department.

Now Mo stepped from behind the lecture stand and walked along the rows of tables, giving a handful of sheets to the first person in each row to pass along to the end. Liam and some of the other members of the department would have chucked the pile down from the dias on to the front table and let the students pass the sheets around for themselves.

The first seat of the back row was occupied by a man who was considerably older than the rest of the students. He sat back from the table, a little out of line with the rest of the row, his arms folded in front of him. When Mo put the final pile of notes on the table he leaned forward, looking for a moment as if he were going to speak, then reached for the papers, managing to look faintly amused without even the suggestion of a smile. 'Thank you,' he said quietly, as he took one set for himself and slid the rest along the table. He settled back a foot or so behind the rest of the students who sat hunched over the notes, and refolded his arms, waiting.

Mo took the class through the hand-out which detailed, week by week, the lecture and seminar topics, then asked for questions. There were none; there usually weren't with first years, they were too used to being told what to do in sixth forms to think of any. Once or twice her eye caught the man at the back who sat, as before, ignoring the notes that the others followed as she spoke, and watched her with the same amused expression on his unsmiling face. There were always one or two students in any new group who stood out in some way. Just a little different in manner from the others – often because they were older, what were known as mature students, and had not come straight from school. Mo did not give it very much thought as she waited for the questions that did not come, and then said, 'I would like you all to write a short paper to bring to me before the first seminar, entitled, "Man's Place in Nature". And I apologize,' she added with a smile, 'for the word "Man". You can assume throughout this course that that word includes both sexes of the human species. But I find "humanity" an emotionally loaded word, and "the human species" is a bit of a mouthful. You're welcome to use any substitute you prefer. We'll read out some of the papers and discuss them in the first week's seminar. Thank you.'

That initial paper always sent small signs of panic around the room, but Mo found it useful because of the preconceptions the essays threw up. It was a simple and fast way of defining the subject, and of revealing the untutored assumptions the students brought with them. After two years of teaching this course, Mo had it down to a fine art. She provided straightforward, basic but useful information for the undergraduates who, for most of the next three years, would be immersed in abstract analyses of social formations. If, from time to time, they remembered that they were talking about a biological species adapting to a physical environment, they might not get so lost in the numerous theoretical alleyways that awaited them.

She shuffled her papers together and left the room as the students began to put their things away and discuss among themselves the daunting prospect of writing an essay on something about which they had never seriously thought. The man at the back of the room slipped his spiral-bound notebook into the pocket of his denim jacket and left the room alone, his footsteps echoing those of Mo who walked a few yards in front of him.

Mo left the department building and headed for the car park. The remarkable weather was a gift, the sun strong and bright and so warm it was impossible to believe they were already in October. She opened the boot of the car and threw in her briefcase next to the overnight bag she had packed that morning in readiness for the weekend she was to spend with her mother. As she wound down the window she noticed the man who had been at the back of the room walking towards the department office. She was glad there was at least one mature student in the group. They often seemed to add a little edge to the seminars.

Four

Marjorie Singleton had just finished laying the table for tea as Mo arrived. When the doorbell rang her hand reached up automatically to touch the side of her hair. She glanced into the mirror above the fireplace, then quickly scanned the table to check that everything was as it should be. Her mouth stretched into a smile as she reached out to open the door.

'Hello darling, how was the drive? You're right on time so you must have missed the traffic.'

Mo's face retained the smile that had appeared as she pressed the doorbell. She leaned forward through the open doorway to kiss her mother on the cheek.

'There's never much traffic at this time of day. You look nice.'

Marjorie was wearing a Liberty-print skirt of tiny blue flowers and a white blouse with a small frill at the collar and cuffs.

'Oh, this weather is so wonderful. We must go for a long walk later, I can't bear to miss a minute of it. It's a gift from God. . . .'

'It's a pity, if God's in such a generous frame of mind, that he doesn't make a present of some rain to the Sahel. Still, I daresay it's pretty for him, up there, looking down on the sunny south of England.'

'Oh, Mo, why not just enjoy it?' Marjorie's eyes took on a slightly pleading quality as she helped her daughter in with her bag.

'I do, Marjorie. It's lovely, but it doesn't stop what's happening in the rest of the world, or me from knowing about it.'

'I wish you could . . .'

'Is something burning?' Mo asked, sniffing.

'The cake! I should have taken it out ten minutes ago,' Marjorie wailed. 'I got involved in laying the table.' She rushed into the kitchen and pulled the cake from the oven. 'I think it'll do, if we cut off the edges. It's probably all right inside.'

Mo sighed as she walked into the smoky kitchen.

'Why don't you buy cakes? I've spent my whole life cutting the edges off your cakes.'

'I'm not very good at it, am I? I never have been. You're right, I don't know why I don't give up and buy the things, but it was always so funny, wasn't it? Do you remember how we laughed, and you and Daddy used to beg me not to make any more?'

'Shall I put the kettle on?' Mo suggested, and busied herself getting the tea ready; warming the pot, measuring tea from the caddy.

'How are things at the university, darling?'

'As ever. Fine.' Mo carried the teapot into the living room and put it with the other things on the table.

'Well, tell me all about your jungle trip,' Marjorie asked as she settled herself and began to pour the tea.

Mo helped herself to a sandwich. 'It was good. Everything went according to plan. I got the information I need, and worked out where the gridding sights will be.'

'I'll miss you. It's such a long time – six months. And on your own.'

'I'll write. And I won't be on my own all the time. There'll be other people at the base camp and I'll have a radio out at the sub-camp. It will be much more efficient doing it alone, less disturbing.'

'But a tropical forest. It's so wild,' Marjorie worried.

Mo sighed. 'Well, that's rather the point of going there, Marjorie. Don't worry, it'll be perfectly all right. I was fine this last trip. Anyway, it's my job, it's what I'm trained for.'

'I know, but it's such a lonely business. Won't you get lonely?'

'I've told you, no. What have you been up to? The garden looks pretty.'

Marjorie sipped her tea from the china cup of cornflower blue that matched her eyes almost exactly.

'Yes, I've been terribly busy with the garden. The weeds are dreadful; the more I pull them up, the stronger they seem to grow. It's a constant struggle. I really can't understand why the things I plant don't grow the way the weeds do. It's very mysterious.'

Mo smiled and took a piece of cake, neatly cutting off the outside with her butter knife.

'Perhaps you should pave it and grow plants in tubs – it might be just as pretty.'

'But I have such a strong picture in my mind of how I want it to look and the weeds spoil it. I bought the most beautiful clematis the other day, but it got the wilt almost as soon as I planted it. Why doesn't bindweed ever get the wilt? The garden's never been quite right since Daddy . . .'

'I'll do some weeding this weekend. Why don't we go to the garden centre tomorrow and buy another clematis?'

'That's a lovely idea. Yes, let's.' Marjorie smiled at the plan, pleased that Mo had suggested it, that they should work together on the garden. She saw so little of her these days with Mo in London working so hard, always busy. And when she came to visit she seemed so tense that Marjorie felt it was an imposition to ask for her assistance with the garden, although Mo was usually there in an emergency. It was just that she seemed so tired that it was hard for the two of them to relax and simply be together, talk about things, the past, plans for the future, what was going on in the village. Mo always got that strained look, those tiny lines at the corner of her eyes and around her mouth, when they talked about things. It made Marjorie very hesitant. The truth was that it was hard for her to remember Mo as a child. It was as if she had always been grown-up and, when she came to think of it, those tiny lines of strain or pain or whatever they were had always been there, even as a very young child, and perhaps even when they had all laughed at the cakes burning. They *had* all laughed, she was sure of that. She had a picture of it clearly in her mind. But perhaps Mo hadn't laughed quite as much as Marjorie and her father. It was hard to remember exactly. It was so long ago.

After tea they went for a walk in the fields beyond the back garden. For the most part they were silent, occasionally commenting on some bit of the landscape. Mo was familiar with all the landmarks, had grown up with the trees and shrubs they passed. A silver birch she remembered as a sapling that had grown along with her; a chestnut tree that had always been solid and towering, whose branches she had climbed and sheltered under; the long grass dotted with cowslips and buttercups that she had flattened as she lay on her back summer after summer watching the movement of the clouds above her head. And the footpath through the meadow, kept open by herself, her family, local people, treading the soil into a permanent track. Maintaining their human right of way through the strangely human habit of 'going for a walk'. The other creatures who inhabited and passed through the fields went with purpose, feeding or finding food, mating or finding mates, sheltering or making shelter. Only the humans walked for the pleasure of walking. Went nowhere in particular then turned about and walked back again. To enjoy the countryside; the right to take pleasure in their surroundings with no other motive beyond the pleasure itself.

Marjorie was quite proprietorial about the meadow and pointed out the old larch that had finally succumbed to the winter frost, leafless and stark amid the greenery.

'Such a pity. It was a lovely old tree.'

The late sun warmed their backs as they walked on.

'I wonder,' Marjorie mused, 'if the trees know that it really ought to be autumn. Do you suppose they're pleased at not having their leaves turn and die? And feel grateful to the sun for the bonus?'

She turned to Mo, smiling with pleasure at the notion.

Mo's hands clenched slightly in the pockets of her jeans.

'Trees don't feel anything. They respond to light and warmth. It doesn't matter to them if their leaves fall or stay on the branches for a few extra weeks. Why do you have to be so sentimental?'

'It was only a thought. If I were a tree . . .'

'You're not a tree. You are conscious, you have language. The

43

natural world doesn't think or feel, it simply reacts to outside stimulus.'

'If you insist,' Marjorie sighed. 'Although I don't see what harm it does to wonder. Why should that larch have died this year and not last year, or next year?'

'Well, I expect it went into a decline because none of its sweet little saplings survived,' Mo laughed.

'Yes, you're right, I'm being silly I suppose,' Marjorie said plaintively, and they walked on in silence.

When they got back they ate supper. Some cold beef that Marjorie had cooked specially the day before. Had overcooked as always, so that it was dark brown and dry, and with it on the plate lettuce and tomatoes, washed and sliced, without dressing. They helped themselves to the triangles of pre-sliced brown bread and butter and finished with tinned peaches and cream. All the tasteless meals of her childhood came back to Mo as she diligently cleared her plate. Not that she minded very much. She was not one for complicated cooking herself, but she remembered the slight smile on her father's face as he had sat opposite her at mealtimes. A gentle humour in his eyes, something wistful, though not unkind, as if he were recalling other plates he had emptied with less duty and more pleasure.

One afternoon she had gone to the library and found a book of French recipes. She sat at the desk for hours, reading it, marvelling at the sauces to be poured over carefully cooked meat and poultry, and the vegetables, barely cooked and tossed lightly in melted butter. The puddings were froths of cream and whites of eggs flavoured with fresh fruit pulp. And herbs and spices to bring out nuances of flavour. She had taken out her notebook and copied down some of the recipes, imagining herself making them for her father and watching his eyes turn from humour to delight as he began to eat. But when she had suggested to him that she make him a meal culled from her careful notes he had hugged her and said no, because Mummy might feel they were criticizing her and they mustn't hurt her feelings.

After supper the two women sat by the unlit fire in the comfortable wing armchairs, as Marjorie embroidered an intricate pattern on a lawn pillowcase and broke the silence from time to time to tell Mo the village gossip. The light died slowly. Mo felt content enough in the familiar room, half listening to her mother's voice, half attending to the country silence, each dependent on the other – silence then sound, and the clock in the hall ticking through both. The cadence of childhood evenings, of being at home.

'I'm almost sorry the weather is so warm,' her mother was saying, head down, concentrating on weaving the needle in and out of the thin fabric. 'It would be nice to have a fire, wouldn't it?'

Mo's peaceful mood broke and a small knot formed low in her abdomen as an old image sprang into her mind, of her mother on her knees in front of the fire, picking woodlice from the blazing logs. Saving them, poor things, from being burned to death, for weren't they living creatures too? If a bird had fallen down the chimney, wouldn't they try to save it? Well, why shouldn't they do the same for the woodlice? One couldn't sit and watch the creatures die just because they were small, just because they were insects.

It drove the adolescent Mo crazy.

'You're not being reasonable, you can't keep everything alive. You kill ants just by walking about, and every time you take a bath millions of bacteria die. Where do you stop?' the high-achieving schoolgirl demanded. 'You'll end up doing nothing at all.'

'But I can't sit here and watch the things die,' her mother would plead.

'Things die all the time. They're supposed to.'

And Mo's father would look up from his book. 'Mo, could you switch on the light, darling? I can't see a thing. Shall we have a cup of tea? Would you, Mo dear?'

Now the adult Mo looked across at her ageing but still pretty mother.

'We don't need a fire, it's fine like this. Shall I turn on the lamp? You'll strain your eyes trying to sew in this light.'

Marjorie went to bed early, kissing Mo on the cheek. 'Good night, darling, it's lovely having you here.'

Mo sat on in the silent room trying to disperse the knot that had formed in her, trying to breathe away the irritation. There was more than thirty year's worth. Sharp fury, knife-edged impatience that had to remain submerged because, after all, no one was to blame, and there was nothing to be gained by giving her mother pain. Her father had explained that to her long ago, when she was barely old enough to understand far less complex things; he had taken her into his confidence and explained about Mummy – the beautiful, floaty, sweet-smelling creature he had made her mother. We must be careful of Mummy, he had told her, we must be kind to her. We . . . we . . . we . . . you and me, darling. She means well and tries so hard. We have to look after her and protect her, because she isn't very good at coping with practical things. But that's all right because she has us to do that for her.

And they did. They made sure that she was not worried by everyday difficulties like paying bills and dealing with the central heating when it broke down, and kept their conversation at the right level when they were all together so that she would not feel they were 'talking over her head'. She was kind and pretty and very loving, and it was easy not to want to hurt her. Mo and her father took long walks in the fields behind the house and he talked to her about his life. The scientist told her about his work and encouraged her interest in the nature of the world around her. And later, in answer to her unspoken queries, he explained about the other woman, the one at the university whom he also loved, but differently. To whom he could talk as he could talk to Mo, with whom he could enjoy concerts, share ideas, and who cooked wonderfully. After the episode at the library he took to describing what they ate, the sauces, the cuts of meat, the wine they drank. Her father's other world that she was not a part of, but was trusted enough to be told about. One day, he promised, they would meet, Mo and Sheila, they would like each other so much.

But he loved her mother too; couldn't help it. Her clever father had fallen in love with enchanting, twenty-year-old Marjorie, with her soft blonde hair and great trusting eyes, and he had not noticed that they talked very little, because they were too busy dancing and laughing and walking in the moonlight. He had looked at her and loved her, and he still did. The love stuck to him like glue, though over the years it had changed until it became indistinguishable from pity, and felt like doom. But it remained; an ache, a pain, a longing; perhaps nothing more than a memory. A powerful trap. He could not leave her.

Except that, all unplanned-for and inconsiderately, he died at forty-five.

Mo mourned him with rage all the busy time during and after his illness: watching his pain, protecting her mother from it, arranging the funeral, dealing with the finances. She kept things going, the practical things, the comfort, and studied hard all the while for her O levels, because he had insisted. He had not needed to say, 'Look after Mummy'; that had been woven into all the minutes of her life.

She hated him in the years after his death; was furious with him for dying and leaving her with the burden of caring for the woman he had chosen to be his wife and so, of necessity, her mother. But having accepted joint responsibility for her long ago, she did what she could to replace him. Not as a husband, of course, but as what he really was – someone who eased the passage of Marjorie's life, who was there when things went wrong, who managed. Marjorie had always had someone there to call on in case of difficulty, and Mo tried her very best not to show her fury, not at being asked to help, but at the incompetence and inefficiency that had driven her mad all her life. Her silly, sweet mother who was now entirely her responsibility.

Mo breathed carefully in her father's old chair, telling herself what a waste of energy it was to feel so angry. It was, after all, only a small part of her life now, she was only called on in an emergency, had only to make brief, regular visits.

She decided to go for a walk, and left the house quietly by the back door, careful not to disturb her mother.

The fields behind the house were shrouded by the moonless night, all the detail Mo had seen during her afternoon walk dissolved now by the darkness into shape and shadow. She climbed the stile, and smelled, rather than felt, the chill October night air. Her mind was on the rainforest project, running over her plans, imagining herself there, analysing and quantifying data, trying to understand the mechanics of an untouched environment. As she thought about her grid of squares, of how she would set them out, it occurred to her briefly that the fields she walked in were themselves bounded, gridded by hedges and fences – although, of course, the scale was much larger – and that she herself walked within the grid, inside a data area. Or would be, if data were collectable on such a scale; or if there were some inhuman-sized scientist capable of collecting it.

The night sounds and the dark held no terror for Mo, who had walked unhurriedly away from the footpath towards the centre of the field. A barn owl hooted, a bat dived and disappeared, small creatures scurried away in the long grass from her predatory footsteps, probably into the waiting jaws of the real predators. It was known territory. Familiar from childhood.

The cicadas buzzed their relentless, pulsing song, the frogs chanted mournfully, and a gibbon howled an endlessly repeated echo into the mist of the approaching dawn.

Mo stopped and shook her head slowly. She had not heard those; not cicadas, nor gibbons, nor the croakings of thousands of frogs. Not here. She closed her eyes and listened hard.

The forest escorted her back to another time in the meadow behind the house. She was twelve and the uncut spring grass and crisp new air made everything bright and light with future. Her father walked beside her and intensified the pleasure of the day.

'Sheila was so pleased to hear how well you did in your exams,' John was saying. They had avoided the path and were wandering aimlessly across the centre of the field. 'She sends her love and congratulations.'

He never kept a photo of Sheila at the house in case Marjorie found it, so Mo had always imposed a face of her own on the Sheila of her mind's eye. Sometimes she looked like the Virgin of Renaissance paintings, a gentle smile of encouragement, an enabling presence. Sometimes she had the strong, intelligent face of Marie Curie (or at least the actress who played her in a film Mo once saw). But most often, as now, Sheila's blank face was filled in with Mo's own, and in her mind she smiled approval at herself for her recent success in the end-of-year exams.

'Why can't I meet her?'

'You will one of these days, darling. But she's so busy, you know how it is. It's difficult.'

Mo thought she understood. If Sheila were quite real to both of them she might be too strong to stay a secret. Some balance would be disturbed. So Sheila, real to John, was filtered back to Mo as a tale told to a deserving child, and lived within their family as a secret shadow. A secret to be shared, but not a solid presence that might divulge itself by being too real.

'Tell me about your visit to the theatre,' Mo asked, sucking on the sweet new grass.

John smiled into Mo's face and she knew he was grateful to her for giving him the opportunity to recreate his time with Sheila. He put an arm around Mo's shoulder and began to describe their evening, starting with her clothes (elegant, understated), then the production (Ibsen, an intelligent, feminist interpretation of *Hedda Gabler*), and dinner afterwards (a good French restaurant in Soho, but still not up to Sheila's cooking).

Mo felt, as she walked inside the curve of his arm, a solid centre of well-being, deep inside her. She was close and contained, feeling his body warmth and heartbeat, smelling his special scent. She adjusted her stride so that nothing disrupted the jigsaw fit of him against her and listened to the rise and fall of his voice, as if it were music and not narrative. She could have her father through Sheila, his memories and pleasure seeping into her across the barrier of skin, a leakage of confused and confusing love. ⸻

Until.

'We ought to get back now. Mummy will have tea ready.'

The place that was filled and blossoming with love deflated and, above it, the anger tightened in her chest. The fist inside her clenched. Holding on, trying for another moment: 'Oh, she won't mind if we're a bit late.'

'No, we mustn't keep Mummy waiting,' John insisted, lifting his arm from her shoulder and ruffling her neat, straight hair to indicate the necessary change in direction and mood. 'It isn't right to keep her waiting.'

Mo knew their time was over, but that it would come again if she kept to all the unspoken rules. The route to her father was circuitous; by collaborating with him over Sheila and Marjorie she could have him back close to her, loving her through them.

'I think it's going to be chocolate cake,' she said conspiratorially as they turned about and headed for the house. John raised his eyebrows in a pantomime of resigned amusement and they both laughed.

'I'll race you to the house,' he shouted, running already. 'Last one back has a second slice.'

Mo, the adult in the midnight meadow, shook her head again and the familiar voice of the barn owl called into the darkness. The long-dead spring and the alien forest sounds evaporated. She had imagined them, she thought, and wondered why. She was not in the habit of imagining things.

In the rainforest a death occurred. One of many in the early dawn. A black eagle swooped and took a pygmy shrew. The shrew felt a searing through its body, but not knowing it as pain, expired, ignorant of its own death. Had it known itself marked as prey by the calculating eyes of the eagle, it would have done what it could to avoid being caught; would have used its instinctive defences against the danger. Could it have chosen, it would have chosen not to die. But as it was, the shrew stopped living, very suddenly and without regret. Nor did the forest mourn the passing of that particle of itself; merely noted an alteration of form. The eagle, being of the forest, partook of a portion of the substance of the shrew, and the rest of it, quite quickly, rejoined the forest as decayed and precious nutrition. Nothing was lost to the whole.

The compound eye of the forest watched, unconcerned, as that part of itself that was Mo stood confused under a northern sky, feeling but not understanding the redistribution of matter that had taken place half a planet away. For Mo herself there was no more than that sense of foreboding she had had when she walked into the dark forest from the light during the summer trip. There was an inner strangeness, a wrenching sense of unfathomable space. It was, she told herself, the darkness. She had somehow lost her bearings in the open field. A kind of agoraphobia, she thought sensibly.

The forest in her knew better but, being locked in behind her language, could do no more than shimmer towards that other forest which observed without intention.

Mo shook her head firmly again and began to walk, trusting in an instinctive sense of direction to return her to the path that led to her back garden, and home.

Once indoors, she went up to her bedroom and began to get undressed. She noticed blood on her pants. 'Damn,' she whispered crossly, realizing she had forgotten to pack tampons in her overnight bag. Her mother, of course, would not have any. She was irritated by her own inefficiency; she had known her period was due. She found some cotton wool in the bathroom cabinet and pulled off a wad that would have to do until she could get to the local shop in the morning. She looked at the soft, white pad with distaste, imagining it as it would be, heavy and wet with the dark, clotted menstrual blood. Before she went to sleep she made an entry in the equipment page of her expedition notebook to remind herself to take plenty of Tampax with her to the rainforest.

Marjorie sat up in her bed, reading a magazine, in the room she had shared with John. It was a pretty, country bedroom, with good but simple furniture that had come to her from her family, and a delicate but fading flower-printed wallpaper. She had made the patchwork quilt that lay over her during a year of evenings, long ago, in front of the fire while John and Mo worked together at the dining table.

She looked forward to the next day when she and Mo would go to the garden centre and choose a clematis. She was particularly pleased that Mo had suggested it and imagined the two of them walking up and down the rows of staked plants, discussing flowering times and the virtue of scent over colour, until the right combination was found. Something that pleased them both and fitted into the overall pattern of the garden. The garden had been John's really, he had made it and developed it. While he was alive Marjorie had enjoyed it, walked in it, or sat in the sunshine admiring the Rosa Mermaid that covered the length of one wall with large, pale yellow petals like sleeping butterflies. The garden was made for her by John and she went into it as a child walks into a room that has been decorated by its parents for its birthday. It was still John's garden; she tried to keep it as he had made it, and always asked herself, before buying and planting anything new or replacing something that had died, what John would have thought.

But it pleased her to think that Mo might take an interest in it. She had been thinking lately that some changes needed making, nothing drastic, but something a little less formal. Perhaps nothing more than curving the edges of the flowerbeds so that there were fewer straight lines. She wasn't sure.

She remembered before she went to sleep that she had wanted to tell Mo about the bad smell that seemed to be coming from underneath the sink, but decided to leave it until tomorrow. It probably wasn't important, and anyway, she didn't want to worry Mo, who always got that funny *brisk* look on her face when Marjorie asked about things like that. She knew Mo didn't mind, but somehow she always felt a little hesitant about asking. She would have dealt with it herself, except that she simply didn't know what one was supposed to do about smells under sinks. A plumber, she supposed, although she didn't know one. But, in any case, it might be something very simple that she hadn't thought of, that didn't need anything as extreme as a plumber. Mo was good at that sort of thing, knowing what was needed, thinking of reasons for things not working, or going wrong. It would be as well to ask.

Five

Mo arrived back at her London flat on Sunday night with a sense of duty done. The clematis had been bought after much discussion – which she knew was the point – and planted. Weeds had been pulled and something appropriately caustic had been purchased to clear the kitchen sink. If it failed, Mo had found the name of a local plumber whom Marjorie promised to call if necessary. Mo did not know whether he was a 'good' or a 'bad' plumber, but Marjorie seemed content that Mo, having picked his name from the local paper, had in some way guaranteed the outcome.

Mo checked into the department office the next morning and found several of the first-year essays waiting in her pigeonhole. She had the morning free and settled in her office to read them over. They were all carefully handwritten on ruled A4 exercise paper, except one, which was scrawled almost illegibly on both sides of two small sheets ripped from a spiral-bound notebook. The corner had been turned down to hold them together, and three horizontal creases suggested it had been folded to fit into a wallet or narrow pocket. It was headed, 'Man's Place in Nature' and the name, J. A. Yates, was half-hidden by the folded corner on the right-hand side. Mo poured herself a cup of coffee and sat at her desk, pencil poised to read what J. A. Yates, whoever he or she was, had to say about the state of the world, since that was inevitably what these essays amounted to. The first line immediately brought to Mo's mind an image of the unsmiling man at the back of the lecture hall.

'Man has no place in nature.'

Mo sipped her coffee and read on.

   'There is no nature, only Nature – an imaginary state of man's

54

own invention, a realm of concept and language. That is man's place and it is nowhere except inside his head; a mirror image of a distorted fantasy he calls Mankind. A distortion of a distortion, exponentially phantasmagorical. Nature is a conceit: a man-made garden in which we wander to relax and preen, as we nod to one another in passing, and congratulate ourselves on being us. We created Nature so that we might take pride in how far we have ventured beyond it.

'Man has no place in nature because there *is* no nature: only what he makes. He is therefore beyond nothing. He is merely self-deceived. Forever trapped inside his self-inflated dream of what he is. A pathetic child imagining himself in the world, when, in reality, he is confined by the four walls of his playroom. His 'world' being nothing more than the arrangement of his diminutive models and playthings.

'Man is exiled from the real world, from nature, by language. He is the willing prisoner of words. All his high-mindedness, his ideals, morality, stemming merely from the necessity of language. True nature cares for nothing, neither life nor death. It is simply in a perpetual motion of growth and decay, beyond value or morality. Lacking the curse of consciousness and the petty ethic that entails, the natural world lives and dies blindly, without intention, regenerates or doesn't. There is no system, only a multiplicity of life cycles; parts that remain separate, that never add up to a whole. Nature does not do arithmetic. Man is one of a myriad of dissociated parts, not outside observer of an illusory unity.

'If he tears down the forests or fights for their preservation, he does it for himself. It is of no consequence to nature, whose disparate parts survive or don't, without sensibility. The 'ecosystem' is man's vision of where he is and, in reality, no system at all. The environment is his own orderly invention, his realm, but the environment cares neither for its own death nor man's. Nor does it care for man's care for it. Man makes a lapdog of a planet in which he is merely a passing formulation of life: the current arrangement of molecules. His continued existence, and that of the planet itself, is of no importance to anything other than the few temporary particles that are our species.

'A few days ago, driving past a hospital, I saw, for a second, a man running towards it with a bundle in his arms. In the moment it took me to pass him, and he me, I saw his face, mouth open. A horrified 'O'. Eyes wide and wild with shock and fear as his legs pumped towards the hospital entrance. The checked rug he held contained a baby. A bundle with a small, pale, indistinguishable face emerging from it. Something had happened, an accident, a convulsion, whatever it is that can happen to infants to make a parent race blindly for help through a busy city street. It was life or death – perhaps. A private disaster.

'There, if anywhere, is man's place in nature. That man at that moment had a place in the natural world. His finite and miniscule tragedy gained him entry. If we touch nature at all, it is through personal catastrophe. Only the death of ourselves or those we feel to be part of ourselves connects us with the planet. The cycle of birth and death and accident is all we have left of nature, and is beyond language and reason. Nature is not an ecologist bewailing the loss of tropical forests, continents and millenia away. It is a child dying in an urban street.'

Mo finished reading and leaned back in her chair, clasping her mug of coffee in both hands.

'Oh Lord,' she murmured to herself as she picked up the phone to dial the number of Liam's room. 'Liam, it's Mo. Would you like a coffee? I've got something I'd like you to see.'

Liam sat in Mo's office reading through the essay as Mo poured his coffee.

'Well,' he sighed, as he placed the sheets of paper on Mo's desk. 'This was written by someone either very young or very dead. Or both,' he added as an afterthought. 'They seem to be dead younger these days.'

'It's not your average first-year essay, is it? I've just checked with the office and they've got no record of a J. A. Yates in the first year.'

'Marvellous. A mystery. Just what we need in this dull, deadly place.' Liam rubbed his hands happily together.

'It's probably just a clerical error, don't get too excited.'

'Why will you spoil everything? Anyway, he sounds like trouble to me. Can't stand these young men who are tired of life as soon as they're out of nappies. That's the prerogative of ageing failures like myself. I don't like competition. Serves you right, though, for setting an old chestnut like "Man's Place in Nature".'

'It's supposed to get all the other old chestnuts out of the way. It's a deck-clearing essay. I didn't expect a Nietzschian tract. Well, I suppose we'll find out who he is at the seminar next week.'

Liam drank down the last of his coffee and then wagged a finger at Mo. 'Better be careful he doesn't have you blowing up the department, my dear. These young iconoclasts can be very persuasive, especially with serious young women like yourself.'

Mo laughed. 'Just because you work so hard on your stereotype doesn't mean the rest of us have to conform. I think I can hold my own against the lad. You know how it is with young iconoclasts, despair is only skin-deep. He probably just read something. By the time I get to see him he'll have read something else and be full of love for humanity.'

'I know how it is with thirty-year-old women too, my dear. Why aren't you married to a bright young ornithologist?' Liam shook his head and blinked at her.

'Because I don't happen to be a character in the novel you're probably secretly writing. Anyway, I'm in love with you.'

'God, how did you know about the novel? If you aren't careful

Liam the Bold will tear away this dour – but false – exterior, and disarray you utterly.'

Mo pulled a face that suggested she wasn't too hopeful of such an event.

'Are you really writing a novel, Liam?'

'No. Yes. No. I'm thinking about it. I'm always thinking about it. Don't change the subject; do you have a lover?'

'As a matter of fact I do. A boyfriend. We go to concerts and films, and sometimes, for your information, he stays the night. He's not an ornithologist, he's a biochemist.'

'Oh, Christ.'

'Well, it's true, he doesn't make bells ring and the sun explode inside my head. But he's nice and we get along very well. I think for most of the world suns don't explode, except in the movies – and inside your romantic old head.'

'One has to believe in something, my dear. Even our young iconoclast believes in something – Nothingness, I daresay,' Liam muttered gloomily. 'Oh, the tediousness of it all.'

Mo pulled her notepad towards her and picked up a pen. 'Yes, it's a comfort, isn't it? Now, run along, I've got some work to do. I'll let you know all about Mr Being-and-Nothingness as soon as I've found out who he is.'

Liam got up and kissed her on the cheek. 'Do me a favour, Little Mo, and fall in love with him, will you? It'll do you both a power of good.'

'Can't,' she replied without looking up. 'I've told you, I have this hopeless passion for you; the way I see it, if you keep on producing babies with Sophie, you'll end up coming to me for a bit of a rest.'

'Don't joke about it, you never know.' He circled the air with his arm in farewell and left Mo making notes for a forthcoming lecture.

Later that afternoon she received a call from Mike, the head of department. 'Can you pop into my office for a second, Mo? I want you to meet your replacement for next term, while you're on your field trip.'

She was less surprised than she thought she ought to have been to find that her replacement for the following term was the man who had sat at the back of the lecture the previous Friday. But she was a little irritated when it came to the introductions.

'Mo, this is Joe Yates. He'll be taking your paleoanthropology course with the first years next term. He said he sat in on one of your lectures last week and was very impressed.'

Joe got up from his chair with an easy smile and extended his hand towards her. Mo took it briefly and turned to Mike. She could feel the flush that was rising angrily to her face.

'Yes, I noticed him.' She turned back to Joe. 'Nice to meet you. I found your essay interesting.'

Joe looked sheepishly at her through thick lashes. 'I'm sorry, I couldn't resist it. Did I get an A?'

'As a first year you get an A minus, but as a lecturer I think you'd better mark it yourself.'

Mike wasn't listening, he wanted to get on with sorting out the admin now that a decision had been made. 'Joe's writing his doctorate. He'll be around this term taking a few of your classes, and then he'll take over your timetable for the rest of the year after Easter. Perhaps you two could meet and sort out the details. Let me know if there are any problems.'

He shook Joe's hand firmly and smiled vaguely at Mo, and they both left him to attend to departmental organization. When they were out of the building Joe suggested a coffee, and they headed for the cafeteria nearby.

Mo sat alone at a plastic table amid the clatter and bustle of the main student restaurant, while Joe fetched coffee from the counter. People of all ages and races sat eating and drinking, deep in discussion or buried in books. Behind Mo, a girl's voice rose and fell in whispered distress. 'I thought I loved him . . . really . . . well, I *did* love him . . .' Then a sentence was lost until her voice rose again out of the general babble. '. . . but I don't want him to be hurt . . .' Her male companion's voice faded in midway through his reply. '. . . expect you to be with him forever . . . about us . . .' Somewhere to the left of her Mo heard a heavily accented voice expounding the course of scientific revolutions. '. . . Kuhn makes quite clear . . . in the discourse of normal science . . . the current paradigm . . . and even if Einstein *said* he was standing on the shoulders of Newton, it's obvious that . . .' An American voice responded, 'Sure, but from the post-structuralist position . . .'

And Mo stopped listening.

Jo came towards her table carrying a tray with two coffees and what looked like a small packet of plastic-wrapped biscuits. He was not very tall, but quite thickly built, with strong, wide shoulders. He wore a dark shirt under a muted Fair Isle jumper that looked as if it had been hand-knitted, and a well-worn leather jacket over cord jeans. The clothes looked comfortable and right on him, Mo thought as he arrived at the table, smiling slightly, and began to unload the tray. In spite of her annoyance about the essay, she was interested in him.

'I got some very dull-looking biscuits for us to have with the coffee, but compared to the cakes they had on offer . . .'

'It's all right. I don't want to eat anyway.' Mo pulled her cup towards her as he sat on the chair at one end of the table. He stirred his coffee, waiting for her to say something, quite relaxed in the silence between them. He was in his early thirties, she supposed, although his round, well-fleshed face was creased with more decades than he could have lived. He was not at all handsome, more nearly ugly, but his wide mouth and pale blue eyes acted powerfully together to paint expressions on his face that shaded from moment to moment imperceptibly into one another. It was a face to be searched for meaning that continually escaped definition. Just as Mo decided on 'disdain', she would see it was actually humour. And then, no, more like anger, or bitterness. It was as if only her perception changed and not his expression at all. His black hair was combed back away from his face, and was a little longer than it needed to be.

'Well, I'm glad Mike's finally sorted someone to take over next term,' Mo began.

'What did you think of my essay?' Joe asked, looking squarely at her.

'I thought it was a bit adolescent. But since it was a joke . . .'

Joe interrupted. 'I meant every word of it. Although I agree the style was a bit high. I expect you think it needed more discipline?' He smiled again and lifted his cup.

'That certainly. You don't seem to have a very high opinion of the human race. Or of ecologists.'

Joe inclined his head in mock disappointment. 'You didn't like it? Then I'll write the other essay – the one about the human race being part of the great holistic Oneness; a cog in the exquisitely meshed gears of the universe, where the miraculous balance of nature is threatened only by villains who run multinationals and use under-arm deodorants.'

Mo retained her self-possession in spite of the anger that was growing. She held her eyes steady as she continued to try a reasoned conversation.

'I found the essay interesting – as I said, for a first-year student – but I don't agree with it. I think we *do* live as part of a balanced natural system, and the evidence seems to support me rather than you.'

Joe laughed gently. 'Well, that's hardly surprising since the evidence is collected by people who are committed to an outcome before they start looking. All I was saying was that human beings need system, so naturally they find it wherever they happen to look. If drosophila were running the planet they'd come up with an entirely different notion of how the world is organized. No one's right or wrong. It's just a matter of perspective and necessity.'

'And your perspective and necessity are not human? You apparently stand outside the illusion the rest of us, according to you, are trapped in.'

Joe shrugged lightly and left a quizzical silence in the air. Mo was uncomfortably aware of having allowed her annoyance to get the better of her. She felt some balance had shifted slightly in his favour.

'What is your thesis on?' Trying to redeem the situation.

'I'm writing up some research I did last year on early human settlements in the Carmargue. It's not terribly interesting. I prefer teaching.'

'Well, I hope you'll be a little careful with the students when you take the classes. They may not be ready for the drama of your opinions. You're taking some of my first-year seminar groups this term, I understand?'

'Don't worry. I'm not out to make converts. I don't care very much whether other people agree with me or not. Anyway, maybe before I'm through you'll have converted me.'

He smiled a large, open grin, though his eyes still held hers with the other kind of humour. Then he sat back in his chair, set at a ninety-degree angle to her, and looked her over, slowly and carefully.

He looked at her with the neutral gaze of an assessor. It was now, clearly, that he would decide if he were attracted to her. And Mo, seeing this, suddenly knew that she wanted him to decide in her favour. She was physically drawn to him, and wanted him to touch her and be close. For the split second during which this process occurred, a sequence of thoughts ran through Mo's mind as fast and as smoothly as if on well-oiled tracks. She wanted him to want her; she wanted to be interesting enough for him to want her. But she feared that he wouldn't, as she watched him take in her neat, summery appearance, and make an overt tour with his eyes of her exterior; beginning at her prim, earnest face and her slightly anxious eyes. Then down, from her tidy, sleeveless front-buttoned blouse and plain blue, straight-cut cotton skirt, to her sturdy naked legs and leather-sandelled feet. She was dressed for the weather, for coolness and convenience, with no thought for style or personal statement. She was discomforted, startled at finding herself now being stared at, subjected to a sexual judgement and, what was worse, finding herself wanting.

When she dressed in the mornings it was without any consideration that she would be looked at like this. Of course, people looked at her all day as she lectured or conducted seminars, but that was, she felt, no more than attention to what she was saying. She did not know how to make the sexual statement she suddenly wanted to make. Neither her clothes nor her body were conditioned to it. Now, she sat in his bold stare and felt exposed, like a plain girl at a dance wearing the wrong dress.

She saw that he had completed his assessment and had decided that he was not interested. She felt dowdy and boring, passed over. And there was nothing she could do, nothing that she knew how to do, that would make any difference.

Yet she had never been that disappointed girl at the dance. Not that she could remember. She hadn't ever tried for that kind of approval in men's eyes. Her sexual life had arisen naturally from friendship and common interest. It was never a specialized activity, separate from the concerts or details of someone's professional life. She could not remember a time when she had exposed her body – naked arms and legs – to fire desire. She hadn't ever been in that market.

The disappointment and confusion lasted for no more than the second it took Joe to run his eyes over her. Then she was angry. Mostly at herself, for wanting something and being foolish enough to feel it was important that she should have it. Long ago she had understood that desire was containable. Of course there had been things she had wanted, that urgent need for something – it did not matter what: a toy, a top mark in an exam, a particular dress, a play, a person. The wanting was always there, a welling need, for a second making you feel as if you would die if you did not have it. Now. But that passed, she had learned. If you did not get it, and held still for a time – and the time decreased as you got more practised at waiting – the urgency went away. It was possible to wait out the wanting and find that one could do without the desired object very well. And once she had learned that, it was easy to go one step further and, knowing she would not want what she wanted eventually, stop herself from wanting it in the first place. You simply made a mental jump in time to the place you would end up. Patience, they had called it when she was a child. And wasn't it the most valuable lesson she had learned? Wait a while, and you'll meet Sheila. Wait, and we'll walk together in the meadow again. Listen to me talk about the woman I love and soon we'll get round to you. And she had learned, in the pause between the wanting and the event, that she could make the ache disappear by not allowing the longing to be felt at all. A very grown-up girl who allowed things to happen or not; who could, by an act of will, not want anything at all, and therefore never be hurt or disappointed when she did not get it.

And as for sexual desire – passion – that was the easiest of all, she thought, feeling stronger, more herself again. No longer the dull girl at the dance. Nothing was easier to deal with than that tenuous, temporary need. She recalled the fragments of conversation she had heard a few moments ago. '. . . thought I loved him . . . didn't love him . . . do love you . . don't . . . do . . . did . . .' You only had to think a couple of stages ahead to know passion for what it was. A cloud, a mist that dissolved as soon as you entered it. Easier to deal with than wanting a bike at that age when everyone else had one.

She looked at Joe as if from a great distance.

'I must go. Thank you for the coffee. I'll see you in college and we can have a chat about the seminars you're taking.' She stood up. 'I hope you won't find it too dull here.'

Joe continued to sit with his coffee, but looked up at her, surprised.

'Not at all. So far it's been very interesting. Why don't we have dinner together? I'd like to talk some more with you about the essay.'

'I'm busy in the evenings,' she said briskly, startled at the invitation. 'We can have coffee one day in the common room.' And she left him, without waiting for an answer, between the guilty couple and the Kuhnians.

*

As Mo left the department that evening for home she bumped into Liam, who asked, as he held the door for both of them, 'Did you find out about your young man, Mr Being-and-Nothingness?'

'Oh, yes,' she replied casually. 'Joe Yates is my replacement for next term. The essay was some kind of prank. It's not interesting at all. I can't wait to get out into the field, I think I've had enough of university life for a while, it's so predictable.'

'I thought predictability was what all you scientific types were after,' Liam said as they stood for a moment in the street.

'There's something to be found out in the rainforest. It's discovering predictability, not knowing it that's the point. 'Night, Liam, love to Sophie.'

Six

Joe was waiting for her when she got home. He sat at the top of the stone steps that led to her front door. As she got out of the car he stood up.

'I thought we might go for a meal,' he called down.

She had not noticed him immediately. It was already dark and his clothing blended into the stonework. She stopped in her tracks and stared. He waved a bottle of wine at her in the silence.

'Or we can just have a drink, if you prefer.'

'What are you doing here? How did you get my address?'

She was confused, startled, rooted to the spot at the foot of the steps.

'Dinner or a drink, as I said. The address, from that very nice secretary in the departmental office.'

'She had no right . . . please go away. I have work to do this evening, and, in any case, I don't . . .'

'Don't what?' he interrupted. 'What don't you do? Eat, drink?'

'I don't mix socially with colleagues,' Mo blurted out, staring up at him.

He laughed. 'That's really very pompous, isn't it? You must be sorry you said that.'

Mo *was* sorry, because it *was* pompous and ridiculous, and had put her, on her own territory, entirely on the defensive.

'You're right, it was a silly thing to say. The point is I have things to do. Perhaps we can have a coffee one day in the canteen at college.'

'But now I'm here, why not have a glass of wine with me? I'd like to have a proper conversation with you. To hear more about the natural system you talked about this afternoon. I'd just like to talk. I don't know many people in London.'

He raised his eyebrows solicitously, and smiled shyly as Mo watched him come down the steps to her side, a lonely man in a new job who wanted company and conversation.

She had a reason now for relenting. He could be allowed in to sit and drink wine and talk. She did not want to be unkind or unreasonable, and he had given her enough excuse, with that shy smile, to feel that that was what she would be if she sent him away now. She could, with him down at street level with her, dismiss from her mind the surge of pleasure she had felt when she recognized him in front of her door. And she could forget that she had had the sudden image, as he waved his bottle of wine, of the two of them side by side on her sofa, and his hand reaching to bring her closer to him. With those unreasoned responses extinguished, she could let him in. There was no reason not to.

'Well, a glass of wine then. But after that you must go, I really do have things to do.'

He nodded assent and followed her back up the steps and through the front door to her flat, where she fumbled with the keys for a moment, and then let them both in.

He told her something of his background over the first glass of wine. He was from Liverpool originally. A bright, working-class boy who, in his late teens, had taken up photography and, admiring the work and, he added ruefully, the life style of the great war photo-journalists, went off to Vietnam when he was little more than twenty. In the footsteps of Capa and McCullen.

'It wasn't nice what I saw. But I clicked away. Snapshots of death.' He shrugged. 'You know the kind of thing. You must have seen them in the colour supplements. Anyway I came home a little crazed. Everyone went home a little crazed. Those that got home.'

He spoke quietly, sitting in the armchair opposite Mo, relating events in a voice without emotion, his solid presence and quiet clothing denying the mayhem that lay behind his words. Only his compellingly unhandsome face and the slightly too long hair

67

suggested he had ever been anywhere at all. He refilled his glass and topped up Mo's.

'I was left with some bad images of the human race. Of what we were. Eventually I decided to start at the other end, and went to university to study paleoanthropology. You know, beginnings rather than ends.'

'And that helped you?' Mo asked, approving of his route.

'No. It provided a few unsatisfactory speculations, but not help. But it gave me something to do, I suppose. And here I am, doing it.'

'A purpose? Something to commit yourself to?'

Joe shook his head disbelievingly at Mo. 'Something to fill in time. A way of relieving the boredom a little. If you must have a neat ending, a moral that I've discovered in my travels, it's that three score years and ten is a hell of a long stretch for a creature with the misfortune to have a sense of time.'

He settled back in his chair and shaded his eyes with one hand.

'Human life is boring. Not just modern industrial life. You've studied anthropology. How does your "natural" man live? He fills about four hours a day with fishing, or hunting or building the odd canoe, then – nothing. The poor sod sits around brewing beer or chewing cocoa to pass the time, just like we watch TV, or go to the movies, or fuck more often than we need to. We're doomed, as we hit the light, to the tedium of seventy-odd years of existence. So what do we do? We invent excitement, something to do. It's called cultural evolution. That's the edge we've got over the rest of nature. Progress, machines, work, duty, family. The whole business, just to keep us going all the long boring time. Of course, the irony is that attempting to keep ourselves busy has just made things worse. We've sentenced ourselves to extra time. They've learned to keep us alive *longer*, for Christ's sake, and so we have to find new ways of staving off the boredom. Mice on a treadmill.'

He rested his case with a wave of his arm that spilled some of the wine from his glass on to the carpet.

'That's nonsense,' Mo said, as she got up and fetched a drum of salt from the kitchen and poured it over the stain. 'The evolution of the human race has been an increasing awareness of inter-dependence. Our sense of time gives us a sense of future generations, a responsibility towards them and the planet. We don't improve life because we're bored, but because we care about what happens to ourselves and our families. The progress you're sneering at is trying to make the world clearer, finding regularities, so that succeeding generations can have more control.'

She returned the drum to the kitchen as she spoke and then sat back in her chair, opposite Joe, who stared down at the little pile of salt at his feet.

'Is this some kind of Dionysian ritual?'

'Salt lifts wine stains,' she explained.

'Did I spill some?' He was amused that she cared about a wine stain on the carpet, an event so trivial that he had not even noticed its occurrence.

'I get it,' he said as understanding dawned, 'you want to ensure the carpet's clean for future generations, right? What crap! Caring about our descendants, preserving the planet. Listen, in thirteen million years a shower of meteors will hit the earth and wipe out the whole race – our successors. The inheritors of our genes will die out. The end. Now tell me, do you care about them? Your great-to-the-power-of-a-hundred grandchildren?'

Mo made an explosive sound of impatience at the idiotic question, and opened her mouth to return the discussion to common sense. But Joe continued.

'So where do you draw the generational line? When do you stop this caring for the future? Two, five, ten generations? Why do you draw a line at all? What has time got to do with caring if it's the race you're caring about? Why aren't you beating your breast about your descendants thirteen million years from now? They're people too – or will be. The point is, the harder you look, the more you realize that we don't care at all – not for them all those generations away, and nor for the great writhing mass of humanity we're sharing the planet with now. The future bit is humbug. We don't give a shit, any of us, beyond expressing the sentiment. Oh, we'll dish out a few quid for the starving millions somewhere across the globe, and worry a bit about the unemployed on the other side of the country. And maybe you'd help out if your next-door neighbour was in trouble. Maybe. If it wasn't too difficult, or inconvenient. You care up to a point. But the point is *you*; proximity to you. Caring is proportional to distance and convenience.'

Mo was furious. 'That's all just romantic rhetoric. You're being emotional. The point is,' she said in the quietly explanatory voice she used for over-excited students in class, 'that we have to preserve resources to ensure any future at all. What we do in the present is about practicalities. Of course individuals can't do much to alleviate what's wrong with the world. Poverty and war are political issues. But the larger issue can't be bogged down by individual suffering. We have to understand the way the system works so that we can control it. If they keep on destroying rainforest and altering climate the human race will die out long before the meteorites hit us. So we have to study our environment, and the more we do, the more we'll understand about ourselves as members of the planet, and that finally will filter down to government policy. That's what real caring is about. That's what my project is about. To get a clearer picture of rainforest ecology.'

'A clearer picture for what?'

Mo was pleased to be offered the opportunity to get the conversation back to reality, and to talk about her plans.

'It's really data collecting. Very elementary because we've neglected it. I'll be dealing with rates of growth and decay in the forest environment. It's the key to the forest's existence. Once we've worked out the life cycle of the forest we'll be in a better position to make a case for conservation.'

'Of course,' Joe said wearily. 'What will you do, put a fence round it to keep the bad guys out?'

Mo was impatient at his sarcasm. 'You're not suggesting we

should do nothing about people destroying natural environments, are you?'

'Why not? I imagine that they're destroying the rainforest because they need it for something else. What makes a natural environment more important than people's needs?'

'Because in a few years there'll be literally none left. We can't allow millions of years of wilderness to disappear because of people's greed.'

'The way I heard it, most of the destruction is done by landless peasants clearing the forest to grow food. I'd call that necessity, not greed.'

'Well, obviously, it's the government that's at fault,' she said uneasily; she was not used to justifying her position like this. 'There's got to be political change. I'm not blaming people who can't help it, but in the meantime . . .'

Joe leaned forward and interrupted. 'You know, it's people that's your trouble. The human race. Us. Let me tell you about the human race, Mo. Somehow that aspect of your education got neglected. It's long since been proven that we are the kind of creatures that destroy rainforest – and anything else we happen to see that we want. That's what we are. We are the kind of creature that looks at a lump of stone and sees a potential axe inside it, so that we chip away at it until it isn't a lump of stone any more, but an axe.' He sliced the air with the side of his hand repeatedly. 'And the reason we spent so much time and effort turning the stone into an axe was because there was a tree in our path, and we needed something that would get it out of our way. If you want to save the world from the ravages of the human race, you've got to get back to before we began to pick the stones up off the ground and look at them in that peculiar, knowing way we have. Do that, and the world becomes a paradise: nothing and no one dies, except by accident and disease; everyone has enough food, because if there isn't enough the surplus population starves and we get back to equilibrium; and there's no politics to bore us all to death, because until an axe is seen in a stone there's no language, and without that we're as good and kind and harmonious as the rest of the natural world. But you're too late, Mo. The stone's long since been picked up. You can't yell "stop", just because the human race has got round to rainforests and you've got a soft spot for them. After all, the only reason why you can go off and make your measurements is because generations of humans have over-exploited the planet's resources to get you to the point where you can judge it a bad thing. Of course we'll fuck up the world – we're human beings. And if we refuse to acknowledge it, we'll fuck it up anyway by misrepresenting ourselves to ourselves. We tell ourselves lies about what we are. We're a dying race on a living planet. We'll go to extinction, like the mastodon, the dodo and rainforests, but we'll probably take the planet with us. So what? It's a natural process.'

Mo refilled her wine glass as he spoke. She hated this kind of fervent nonsense. He stared curiously at her with his strong blue eyes.

'According to your essay, we're completely alienated from nature. Now you're saying that we're innately destructive, biologically determined to wipe everything out because we see axes in stones.'

'You weren't listening.' He lit a cigarette and looked around the room for an ashtray. Mo got him a saucer from the kitchen as he continued. 'It isn't seeing axes in stones; it's seeing the tree in our path as a problem that can be solved by cutting it down. It's the *need* for the axe that has doomed us. The natural world would walk round the tree, not think about it. Our problem is that we can think. And worse than that, we can think about ourselves and what we want. That overrides everything else. Our biological origins are irrelevant once that has happened. There's nothing to be done about it. If we choose to think how to get our desires, or refuse to think how to get them, it makes no difference. We are completely alienated on this planet. Things apart. The fact that the choice to think is available puts us forever outside natural behaviour. Self-awareness is what turns us into killers and wreckers.'

Mo returned to her chair. 'You too?'

He ran his hand over his forehead and through his dark hair, and laughed sharply. 'Certainly, me too. More than most. I've done my share of wrecking. I've seen forests destroyed and living things burned to death. Let me put that more accurately: I have personally participated in the destruction and death-making. You can't *just* take photos in the middle of a jungle war. If you want to know about the human race, you're talking to an expert.' He sat back again, and the old sardonic smile returned. 'So why don't you just fence in a small patch of forest that you can make pretty patterns on and measure, and let everyone else get on with making whatever living they can, while they can. And don't worry about the grandchildren,' he added, 'we've got plenty of TV documentaries in the archives we can show them. If there are any.'

Mo stared at him. His overall manner was aloof, the voice sneering. But for a fraction of a second when he talked about his time in Vietnam, the brilliant blue eyes narrowed and lost their remoteness. It was hardly noticeable, no more than a flicker of tension between his brows that vanished in an instant.

'I'm sorry,' Mo said, nervous and uncertain at the injection of his pain into the conversation. 'It must have been terrible, being there.'

'Forget it.' He glared at her angrily. 'I don't want to talk about it, especially not with well-brought up lady academics. And don't start to fucking analyse me, either.'

Mo opened her mouth to say something, but he stopped her with a stab of his finger into the air between them.

'Nothing!' he snapped. 'Not a word!'

There was a strained silence while he stubbed out his cigarette and placed the saucer on the floor. Then he relaxed back into the chair and crossed his legs, his self-possession completely regained.

'You're a hypocrite, Mo,' he said with a lazy grin. 'You're going off to study rainforests because that's your way of finding something to do with your time. It suits your temperament to sit in the middle of nowhere looking for order. If you hadn't had an academic brain you'd have been just as happy being a professional wine stain remover. You're just a neat person tidying up the world. I've seen your office and listened to you lecturing, and watched you pouring salt on the carpet. There's no great meaning in what you're doing. You're just pissing around like the rest of us time-wasters.'

Mo flushed. In the first place, he was wrong. In the second, he had manoeuvered the conversation from the general to a personal confrontation and created a change of pressure. The air itself seemed altered between them. A shift that she had been quite unprepared for had suddenly and unexpectedly taken place.

'Look, I'm not very interested in your assessment of my character. And, as I said, I've got work to do . . .'

Joe leaned forward again. 'Let's go to bed.'

Mo's spine went rigid.

'I don't . . .'

'I know – mix socially with colleagues.' He stood up. 'I'd like to fuck you, but I'll go if that's what you want.'

Mo stared up at him for a long moment.

She heard the front door shut, looked around the empty room with its echoing silence and experienced a long, slow night of regret, while Joe stood beside her chair waiting for her decision.

'Thank you,' she said coldly. 'But I'm not interested.'

Joe shrugged slightly. 'OK. See you in college.'

She heard the front door shut and sat still in the empty room.

There was regret. She *had* wanted him. Beside the conversation had run her continuous awareness of his physical presence, strong, reined in, but there, very real in the room. She had taken him in with her eyes while her ears received his words, and her body had responded, quietly but insistently. She knew that now, because his absence caused an ache of disappointment, and her need for him punished her in the silence. It was purely physical. He had insinuated sexuality into the room and left it hanging there with his departure. She was not used to this; to being confronted like this. To being offered sex, and wanting to take it. She sat through the hours, reading, making notes for lectures, trying to dismiss the desire that would not go away as easily as Joe had.

She and the biochemist, Luke, had known each other for a month before they had slept together. They had eaten with each other, shared ideas, accompanied one another to concerts, the theatre. Never intense, always pleasant: their relationship, their sex. There had never been a Joe Yates in her life who came through the door and said, 'Let's go to bed.'

For a moment her mood altered, and there was the sharp, rebellious fury she had suppressed so often when she was young. Why did she have to deny herself what she wanted? Why shouldn't she, couldn't she, have said yes? She recognized the anger and wondered for a second what it was she had wanted as a girl that had been so impossible. For a moment, had she had Joe's phone number, the rebellion would have won. Why shouldn't I, she muttered angrily, why shouldn't I?

But there wasn't anything she could do about it, and the night passed, as it inevitably would have, whatever had happened.

Joe walked home through the dark streets to his room in Chalk Farm. He wasn't greatly put out by Mo's refusal. He had offered more out of curiosity than anything. He wasn't especially attracted to Mo, but he was intrigued by her plainness. He wanted to take off her uninviting clothes and, with them, her uninviting manner, and see what happened when they, and her remorseless blandness, were challenged, body to body. He had wanted to chip away a little at her exterior and see what happened when she stood naked and was obliged to exchange reasonableness for sexuality. It was interesting to see what people were when their clothes were off and made vulnerable by the sudden redundancy of language. But, he thought, as he pulled off his own clothes and dropped them by his bed, there were some who wouldn't take them off, and that was an answer in itself. His curiosity wasn't so great that it could not be satisfied with that. And he was asleep immediately, his arms flung wide across the bed, like a child who had nothing to fear from unconsciousness and the night.

75

Seven

Another dream last night. I wonder if the forest will ever leave me be, whatever Dr Taylor may say about time. It's strange how creature-like it has become since I left it. I'm no animist, I've never cluttered up the environment with *personality*. It is extraordinary how unconnected dreams can be from reality.

Last night the forest breathed. I dreamed I was walking through the forest, trudging over the debris and rotting vegetation of the undergrowth, shouldering my way past the looping creepers and tangled shrubs that push upwards in their search for light. Suddenly, I saw a shaft of light ahead of me; hardly light as one would recognize it outside the deep gloom of the forest interior, little more than twilight, a faintly golden haze that got its definition only from the surrounding darkness. There had been a tree-fall and a great ficus lay on its side. I could just make out the shape of one of its giant buttresses, lying like a fin in a sea of sun-dappled green shoots and leaves; the new growth that had sprung greedily into existence, each stem and sapling grasping its chance for life, fighting for height and strength to fill the space left by the ancient fig; to close the gap in the sky. I began to walk towards the pool of light, wanting to investigate, when I heard a sound behind me, so unnatural to the place I stopped and turned around. For an instant I saw a figure some fifteen feet away, or thought I did, but as I stared, it seemed to break up and melt into the forms of the forest, becoming no more than the edge of a leaf, an angle between branch and trunk, the shadow of a spathe. As I watched, the sound came again, silencing to my ear the rest of the forest's chatterings. A long exhalation like a profound sigh. And this time it came from a different direction, then another and another. Deep, sonorous breathing, amplified and sexless.

I tried to move forward to reach the light, but the sound pulled at me like gravity, first this way, then that, and I was held fast. The breathing pinned me as if invisible ropes had been flung about me from all directions, holding me tighter with each inhalation, clinging, rooting me to the spot. As I looked towards the light, no longer trying to reach it – I saw that the new growth around the fallen tree had speeded up impossibly and was now racing madly to fill the gap in the canopy. Stems and trunks thickened with every second as saplings became soaring trees, and creepers twined thickly around them, like muscular arms trying to grasp the last chinks of light overhead.

Then darkness fell where the light had been, and the place became one with the rest of the forest. There was no more direction. No *there* any different to *here*, and I was as content to be where I was as anywhere else. I stood quite still, not needing to be held in place, and felt, as I listened to the regular breathing and looked into the undifferentiated forest, a great satisfaction that it had returned to itself, enclosed again in a proper darkness.

The dream stayed with me all day, hovering around the edges of my mind. The quality of the dream remained like the smell of smoke after a fire has been extinguished. I tried to work my way through it, to proceed as normal, but I couldn't quite get clear of it.

Today it was the Dwyer house in Islington. I set off at nine, as usual, to catch the bus, but I felt heavy, full of forest. It had rained in the night and the clouds were weighted overhead with more to come. I closed my front door and walked down the steps to the wet pavement, feeling the damp beneath my plimsolls. I don't generally mind the wet and cold; I find if you don't give a value to them, they become simply *conditions*, no better or worse than anything else. You can cut away the *feeling* cold, and be left with nothing more than a description of the temperature of one's skin. But this morning the quality of light seemed to matter. The dark sky washed the concrete and brick of the streets a dull yellow and the whole city became a vast Victorian institution; all corridors and waiting rooms. A maze with no centre.

Of course it was just the residue of a restless night, and I tried to keep my sense of discomfort at bay, to remember it for what it was. Not important. Still, the Dwyer house felt like a refuge as I closed the door behind me. A place of safety. I went straight to the kitchen to sort out the cleaning equipment, and felt immediately better at the sight of its gleaming white surfaces and clean, straight lines. Everything fits, edge to edge. It is a laboratory for the processing of food, with everything flush and flat to conceal the machines that do the work. It looks empty, as if it were nothing more than a series of smooth planes, all pure white in contrast to the black rubber floor.

It seemed to smooth away the density of my dream, and I relaxed as I filled a square, white bucket with hot, soapy water and took it expectantly into the living room.

It makes me gasp a little every time I see it. I stand for a few minutes in the doorway taking it in. The ceiling and three of the walls are white; the fourth, the one facing me, is painted matt black and seems to rise, like a shadow, from the shiny black vinyl flooring. It is a large room, and almost empty. In the dead centre, two black leather Eames chairs face each other on either side of a white flokati rug, on which is a black metal trolley holding a small pile of glossy magazines, and a glass rose, laid casually at an angle. To my left, against the wall, is a structure, built, as far as I can see, of scaffolding, also black, which houses machines for sound, vision and recording, all neat cubes of black plastic and winking red lights. The light fittings are the kind you see in pictures of professional photographic studios, with complicated shutters and reflectors to angle the beam this way or that. There is nothing else in this extraordinary room. Sometimes I try to imagine Fanny and Jerome sitting opposite each other in their Eames chairs and feel a slight urge to laugh, but must admire them; a room like this demands such discipline from the living.

It is my job to retain its empty, over-styled perfection. It would be disfigured by the slightest film of dust. The clarity of my task pleases me. The floor must be wiped and shined; the surfaces sprayed with anti-static polish; the windows, with their narrow, black Venetian blinds, must gleam through the slats. And then the room, pristine as I close the door behind me, is perfect, like a church without God.

Sadly it seems, this vogue is nearing its end. The components of the room are beginning to appear in High Street furniture stores, and photographs of rooms similar to this in their catalogues. Fanny told me recently that they were calling in an interior decorator to redesign the house. She says she feels it ought to reflect its Georgian origins. So I will not be working here for very much longer. I want to remember it as it is now and, in any case, I couldn't work in the disruption that the alterations will involve.

Nick phoned this evening. He had been planning to come round, but called to say he couldn't because he had some important new notes to write up.

'It's about entropy,' he said, his voice sounding stretched. 'That's where it all comes together. The Second Law of Thermodynamics.'

'All matter tends towards increasing disorganization?' I intoned, dredging up my school physics.

'Yes, right. An irreversible progress towards chaos and death. But suppose it isn't? Irreversible, I mean. Suppose it's part of a greater process? Chaos as process. Do you see what I mean?'

'No.' I could imagine him hunched intensely over the phone, one hand clutching the receiver, the other massaging his temples.

'Look,' with an attempt at patience, 'think of a system in equilibrium. An orderly system. It goes on and functions for a while. Then something happens. Something from outside upsets the balance. The thing goes out of whack. It's not stable any more. That's when it begins to move towards disorganization. It won't function. It goes towards chaos. But suppose instead of becoming disordered and useless it takes on another form. A new structure emerges. Not chaos. A *different* structure. Do you see now? It's a matter of pure chance, it *could* become useless and chaotic, *or* it could become something else, that functions in another way. So that through the disruption of order is a new order. Instead of inevitable death, you get evolution.'

'Yes,' I said hesitantly.'That makes sense, in theory. But I thought the entire universe was subject to entropy. Are you saying it isn't?'

'Disorder is the most probable state. You can predict it with near certainty, and once you've got it, it's an indefinite state. With a system with a multitude of parts, the most probable arrangement of those parts is chaos, statistically. Well, you can order the system for a time, but time is the problem, you see. As the orderly system works, it decays into disorder. So by ordering the system, you're actually creating disorder. In the end you get more disorder than order out of it.'

'Nick, I can't cope. What does all this mean?' I knew he was trying to get something clear in his head, to pull together pages of jumbled and scribbled notes and diagrams, through explaining it to me. I didn't feel I was being very helpful.

'I'm saying that there's a system above what we think of as the inevitable law of increasing entropy. A system that uses our system as part of its process. Our system is only a subsystem. Chaos isn't the end point, but a stage in a much larger movement of change. Because we're locked into time, we're on a point on the line, so we can't see the larger mechanism, just as we can't see the whole of the milky way, because we're part of it. This isn't crazy, Mo. This is the stuff of everyday physics.'

As he spoke I got a picture in my mind of the Dwyer living room. I couldn't imagine that fierce order degenerating into chaos. It wasn't in a state of flux. Except that Fanny was getting in the decorators. Fanny was the outside, disturbing force that would tip the system into chaos, or, in this case, a new order. Personally, I like things to stay as they are. Universal entropy or not. And I certainly don't see why people like Fanny have to help the universal process along. I didn't think Nick would appreciate my simplistic view of the new physics.

'You're saying that there isn't chaos, but there is change? Is that it?'

'Yes, ultimately. But it's impossible for us to get outside the system enough to observe it.'

'Well,' I muttered, feeling very tired, 'if it feels like chaos, then it is chaos as far as I'm concerned. It's like postulating an afterlife. It's too speculative to be useful. We have to deal with what there is. We can't imagine what we can't imagine. If truth is outside what our brain structure can handle, then it's the same as if there were no truth – at least for those of us with ordinary brains.'

'That's the point of my book, Mo,' Nick explained patiently. 'The new physics points a way beyond the limits of our perception. We have to develop ways of getting outside the pattern of our brains. There are other systems of thought, going back millenia, that refer to what physics is only just discovering. The ancient sages were actually physicists.'

I sighed quietly. 'Look Nick, it isn't that this doesn't make some kind of sense. But do you think you ought to be doing this? I just wonder if it's not too much of a strain . . .'

Nick sounded tense. 'I'm fine. This is important work, Mo. I know it's what I have to be doing.'

'All right,' I answered hastily, and suggested he come round tomorrow evening. He said he would, and we were still friends when we put the phone down.

I wonder if it's really Nick's mental health that concerns me most, or if it isn't the discomfort I feel at listening to his hypotheses. He formulates the theory of what I once lived through. Or thought I did. At any rate, it reminds me of things I would rather not think about.

I live well enough now, without complexity, without going over and over what . . . may have happened. I avoid reminders. Nick doesn't know what his ideas bring me closer to. It's not his fault. I have to listen and encourage, because he needs it, but actually I reject it all utterly. I don't care whether it's true or not. I don't want to know. I've got my life working again – I cope. I'm competent. I get through the time by making one thing follow another. A simple line of events, of time. My life is a list of things to do, and my satisfaction is in doing them well. I don't want anything else. Above all, I don't want speculation.

Dr Taylor suggests with great delicacy that there is something unresolved in me. Some pain I won't admit, won't feel. But I reject that notion too. So what if I'm not 'happy'? *Happy* and *sad* seem to me like the wet and cold of this morning. Conditions to which you can choose to give a value or not. The point is that my life works. I function; I'm not a cripple. There is nothing I yearn to do that my 'sadness', as he calls it, prevents me from doing. I do not believe in the depths, the sub-consciousness, that Dr Taylor's profession requires him to believe in. If it's there, it doesn't hamper me in my practical life, and therefore I don't need to dredge it up. I am who I am and my life is all right; I won't put it at risk by brooding.

What happened – then – was an interruption, not an unplayed theme in my life.

There are the dreams, of course, but I'm sure that, eventually, they'll go away. If I just get on with things, they'll stop. I'm quite sure of that. And anyway, truth is a dangerous business. If there is some overarching truth that Nick is working towards, it requires, I should imagine, great stability in the person who perceives it. Nick doesn't have that. I know my limitations.

Eight

Autumn set in with a vengeance in the first week of November. Trees that had been swathed in green turned yellow, then brown, seemingly within days. The air had a touch of ice about it, and the lights had to be turned on in the seminar and lecture rooms well before the academic day was over. Everyone seemed to be taken by surprise, and remarked to each other about the new season as if it were indeed quite new and unexpected. All the light and bright clothing was shed and the university was now inhabited by people wearing boots and sweaters and thick coloured tights, who kept their heads down against the gusty winds as they crossed the quads and alleyways from one building to another. Students kept their coats on during seminars until the central heating had warmed them sufficiently to shrug them over the back of their chairs, and the hardier ones called for a window to be opened against the offending smoke and fug that built up.

Mo rather liked the winter. Liked to pull an Aran sweater over her brushed-cotton shirt, and wear thick socks inside her boots. She found it pleasing to finish a lecture and come out to find it suddenly dark, with that smoky, frosty smell in the London air, and the warm, bright lights of the bookshop around the corner, welcoming, indicating that it was still open for business and that the day was not yet over. She did not, once it had arrived, object to the season at all.

She continued to teach her courses and run her seminars with her usual efficiency that term. She visited her mother a couple of times, and saw Luke, the biochemist, once a week or so. It was all as normal. Only Liam thought he detected something different about Mo; no more than a slight tension, and something that looked like pain flashing across her eyes very occasionally. He watched her more carefully, but said nothing. When he dropped in to her room for coffee and a chat, the talk was mostly about himself.

'It's no good, Mo, I can't abide this dark, God-forsaken, northern country,' he would complain. 'There is no light. No inner light. We're all termites, scurrying about in the dark, rebuilding our nest to make sure the light will never get in. Can I come with you to your forest?'

'It's just as dark there. Light activates the pineal gland, you know. That's why we're all so dour in the northern hemisphere. But if it's any comfort, there's enough light even on a completely overcast day to keep cheerful. You have to get out more. An hour a day at least. You spend too much time indoors.'

'You're so practical. The idea of going for daily walks to keep my pineal gland active is very depressing. The fact is that God doesn't visit cloudy countries. He likes wide open spaces, bathed in sunlight. He sends us his emissary – a practical angel who keeps things tick tick ticking over. But he doesn't have the luminosity of God. I need God, not his wretched henchman.'

'I thought Sophie and the kids had luminosity.' Mo sipped her coffee and smiled.

'You will keep harping on how happy I am.' He blinked decisively. 'Don't you see, that has nothing to do with it. What has loving your wife and kids got to do with being banished from the garden?'

'Everything, I should have thought,' Mo answered briskly. 'At any rate, it's better than nothing.'

'Once you know you've been exiled you are everywhere and always alone. Human love just mocks at you with its incompleteness,' Liam declared, waving his hand to emphasize the hopelessness.

'You're so melodramatic. I hope you don't talk to Sophie like this – she might believe you. As I see it, you and Sophie have got each other and the kids. And you like each other. What more do you want, apart from the pleasure of complaining?'

'Philistine,' Liam retorted, and went on the attack: 'What do you have, Mo?'

'Nothing.' So abruptly that both of them started in surprise. She corrected herself, raking her hair back over her wide forehead with one hand. 'Friendship. My biochemist – go on, sneer if you like. And my work. And you, Liam, to remind me how lucky I am not to be in love with tragedy.'

That conversation again, but Mo's lines said with a new brittleness that sounded less convincing than usual. Liam began to feel the satisfaction that comes to the professionally unhappy when they see neat edges fraying a little.

Mo had not seen Joe since the night he had come to her flat with a bottle of wine. Not socially. They had had a formal meeting to discuss the seminars he was taking, and he had been pleasant enough, listening politely to her suggestions and making notes. He nodded amicably at her when they passed each other in the department. There was nothing personal in their encounters.

The forest embodied in Mo noted the loss of heat and light in the north and added a notion of seasonality to the bank of information it had about its environment. It noted also something more familiar, that it identified as similar to those times when its warm-blooded components lost new life: when a creature whose body had been preparing to give birth produced instead something stillborn, lifeless. When that happened there was incomprehension, confusion. What was to happen had been unknown, yet what did happen was understood as wrong. The organs and glands that had prepared for life were rendered useless, and the creature, lacking an understanding of what had occurred, still felt that things were not right, had not come to a conclusion. Rat, deer or monkey, it would gaze at the dead thing it had produced and feel its body ready to feed and nurture, and not comprehend, or be able to make any connection between the two. It was this sense of an unfinished process that the forest recognized in Mo, and understood, since it was an event that had happened many times. It did not even represent a disruption to the watching eye of the forest, so small and passing a thing it was, merely a recognizable set of responses to be noted. The forest – leaf, liana, shaft of light, termite, monkey – watched and listened to what happened to itself. For this event, no immediate adjustment was needed, the overall pattern of the forest had not been affected by this single, tiny interruption in the continuity of the part of it that was Mo.

Unlike the forest, Mo failed to recognize her condition. At least, she would not give a name to the spasm of discomfort that passed through her from time to time. When it happened, in her diaphragm and across her eyes, she ignored it, telling herself that it was nothing, that it had not happened. She berated herself for feeling what was unreal, an emotional twinge for which she had nothing but contempt. Unlike the forest, she had no sense that something unborn in her had died, and would have scorned, had the thought crossed her mind, the notion that anything so slight, so crude as her passing, passed attraction for Joe could have engendered anything of any importance. He amounted to nothing, it wasn't anything she needed.

As the weeks passed she saw him around the college, arriving one morning with one girl, leaving at the end of another day with a different one. After a while, she began to watch the girls rather than Joe, and found she could discern who had been taken on and who discarded from their posture, the tilt of their head, the way their eyes glanced or did not in his direction. He littered the department with his used-up girls, who took their triumph and dismissal with varying degrees of stoicism. One morning she arrived at the office to see a look in Sally's eye that told her immediately that the departmental secretary was the latest to have won his favour. She waited, interested, for a few days before she saw the other look, a slackening of the muscles around her mouth, a heaviness about her shoulders, that announced Joe had moved on. Sometimes she did not even need to see them. After Sally's fling was over, it was several weeks before the departmental typing was back to its normal standard and the right number of the right originals got photocopied. Sometimes it was a change in tone in a student's seminar papers and essays that indicated the stage she was at in Joe's progress. She watched with fascination, and some disgust that she herself might have in any way participated in the dreary procession, but was glad that *she* had not got involved, or suffered any of the pathetic aftereffects. She had cut him off, fast and efficiently.

But while she was concentrating on the phenomenon of Joe and the mess he made, the polymorphic eye of the forest took in the small disturbance within Mo and noted, for future reference, that the balance of this organism was no less subject to accident and mutation than any other in its composition. The forest whispered this useful information to Mo, though not in any language that she could comprehend. She understood no more than that, occasionally, when she was alone, she experienced a shimmer in the air, a curtain of dancing light that seemed to penetrate the barrier of her skin and create a sense of expectancy. She found herself straining to listen, waiting in the silence, and then wondering what it was she waited for. Usually she resolved these strange moments with thoughts of herself in the rainforest, pacing out the distances for her grid, writing up notes by the light of a gas lamp back at Base Camp, building her picture of the working of the forest from the statistics that would grow into meaningful graphs and distribution curves. She was comforted, when things felt not quite right, by these practical daydreams.

As it turned out, it was Liam who lost his balance.

Suffering as he was, at the end of the Christmas term, from the lack of light and God, he was overcome with an anguish which he attempted to assuage by burying his worried, whiskered face between the smooth breasts of one of the more nubile first-year students. It was, as Mo told him severely when she found him later in his room, head in hand, a confusion of desire, and exactly what happens to people who wallow in emotionality.

It had happened at the end of a seminar. Liam noticed Grace at the beginning of the session as the eight students settled themselves around the table. She was lusciously endowed, and still, apparently, had not caught up with the change in season. Liam asked one of the students to switch on the light against the fading afternoon and as he did so, like a particularly effective *coup de théâtre*, the room glowed a warm yellow, the world beyond the windows faded into twilight, and Grace's pale, filmy blouse became translucent. Liam stared for a moment, transfixed by the naked breasts and nipples beneath the fine gauze, bouncing gently as she shrugged off her jacket and reached into her bag for her notes, then resting plumply on the surface of the table when she stretched across it to take a light for her cigarette. This careless exposure was quite unconscious on Grace's part, as is only possible for a young woman unthinkingly confident in her own naked loveliness. Liam dragged his gaze away from Grace and began the seminar on the topic, carefully chosen with the coming festivities in mind, of The Gift.

He offered cross-cultural and historical evidence for the universal importance of exchange in the fostering and maintenance of social formation, and then threw the subject open for discussion.

'Let us, for example, consider the gifts you might give or receive in the next week or two.' But his eyes kept tracking back to the extraordinarily enticing breasts and, occasionally, to the innocent and concentrated eyes of their owner. 'There are, even in this age of Mammon, still rules of gift-giving that cannot comfortably be flouted. Your parents may, and I daresay will, give you a cheque. But could you give them, or your favourite aunty, a fiver for Christmas? You might, and I'd really rather you didn't, give me a tie. A gesture towards a teacher. But suppose I gave you an article of clothing? If I gave Grace, for example, a nice, warm vest – worried as I am about her catching her death of cold? It would be, would it not, inappropriate?' Liam's face contracted at this moment in an eyeblink which concentrated his features into half their normal area.

Grace reddened and dipped her head so that her wavy, blonde hair hid the rush of blood to her face, as the others around the table laughed merrily at Liam's little joke. They all had parents who, at one time or other, had nagged them to dress sensibly and warmly – advice which, generation after generation, flies in the face of youth and fashion. And having just flown the coop, they enjoyed Liam's parody of toothless authority. For so they understood it, because, although there wasn't a single virgin in the room, they were still too young and sexually innocent to perceive the concealed lust in the eyes and voice of a man old enough to be their father, and a teacher to boot. Liam was camouflaged by their inability to conceive of him as a sexual being.

The mood was light and humorous as they teased apart the familiarity of Christmas to find the common thread of ritual and ceremony that linked this Godless, technological age with primordial groups of barely human creatures who, like contemporary toddlers, held out offerings to one another to signify affinity and relative distance.

At the end of the session Liam summarized: 'Well, we seem to have discovered that there is nothing very new about the way we try to keep in contact with our fellows. It just looks different. Shinier and more metallic. Underneath the acrylic and silicon implants, we're the same old savages. And don't tell anyone else in the department that such a word passed my lips – savage, I mean, not silicon implants – I'd be cashiered.'

The group laughed as they shuffled their things together and left the room, still discussing the anthropological nature of their forthcoming Christmas. Grace, however, took longer than the others to put her things away. Her slowness was obviously intentional, and her lack of hurry might easily have been confused, to one inclined to see things like that, with sensuality. When they were alone in the room Grace, still slipping pages into her folder, said, 'Liam, I wanted a word with you about my essay on the Nature/Culture debate.'

Liam, having nothing else in the room now to distract him, found it almost impossible to keep his eyes from feasting on her cleavage. It felt extraordinarily restful, like staring into the middle distance after a long session of television watching.

'Are you having a problem?' He forced himself to look up to her pretty, but not-yet-quite-defined face.

'Well.' She got up thoughtfully, cradling her file in her arms, and walked around the table. She placed the open file in front of Liam and stood by his side, resting one hand on the desk. 'It's this quote from Lévi-Strauss. I don't really understand.'

Liam looked down at the file and read, '. . . the characteristic of nature is that it can give only what has been received. Heredity expresses this permanence and continuity. However in the sphere of culture, the individual always receives more than he gives, and gives more than he receives.'

'Just another of the old imp's fancies,' Liam said when he finished reading. 'He only does it to annoy, you know.' Grace had bent down over the page; he could feel a wisp of hair brushing the side of his face.

'But how can you give more than you receive, and receive more than you give? It doesn't make sense.'

Liam looked up at her. 'Sense has nothing to do with it, my dear. It depends, rather, on *what* is received and *what* is given, doesn't it? The point is, for your purposes, that nature can only work with what is there, whereas culture can make more and different.' He was not at all interested in Lévi-Strauss, or Grace's essay, for which he had no great hope. Grace at this moment sat down next to Liam, hoping to get a little more specific guidance, and Liam experienced an excruciating spiritual emptiness, as if the stars had focused on his heart and burned it away.

'Grace,' he whispered, as if he were naming the state rather than the person, and turned towards her. She blinked at him and waited for further intelligence. He felt tears spring into his eyes as he continued to try with words.

'You might say that nature represents your beautiful body, but culture clothes it, half obscures it, and makes it all the more desperately desirable.' As he spoke he gazed down at the slope of her breasts and watched hopelessly as his hand slipped inside the V-shaped top of her blouse. Her skin was satiny; the fine cotton on the back of his hand felt rough by comparison. As his fingers found her nipple, it occurred to him that if he could sink his face into those lovely mounds, it would be not unlike a certain ecstatic experience he had had some years before while meditating with a group of dervishes in the Hindu Kush. Grace began to pull away and whispered in a voice much less surprised than he had imagined, 'Liam, don't . . .'

He cupped her breast. 'Please, my dear, please . . .' he begged. 'It's most important.' And then, removing his hand, he buried his overflowing eyes and drooping mouth in the soft flesh.

Grace was very moved that she had caused such deep desire in a man as mature and clever as Liam. It was true she did not find him as physically attractive as the young men she had previously had as lovers, but he made up for that with the depth of his passion. Before she pulled her blouse over her head to reveal nature, stark and uncluttered, she pushed him gently away.

'Don't you think we should lock the door, Liam?'

They made love on the carpet tiles, beneath the blackboard. Once or twice she called out, 'God . . .' breathlessly, mostly in astonishment at the frenzy that was going on above her and inside her. She wondered, for the first time in her sexual career, if it were possible to be damaged in there, as Liam grunted and groaned and wept, and ploughed into her as if he were searching for some concealed entrance to another world. 'Oh, Sophie. Oh, Sophie,' he cried as he came. 'Oh, God. Oh, my love, my love . . .'

When they had rested for a few moments, Grace asked, 'Who's Sophie?'

Liam stared vacantly at her, blinking once or twice, and got up, hurriedly zipping his flies and tucking in his shirt. He ran his hands through his hair and over his beard, as if trying to flatten his sense of sin out of existence.

'Please forgive me,' he said, hardly able to look at her lying on the floor. 'I lost control. I'm desperately sorry. I must go, I'm so sorry.'

He pulled at the door, then remembered, and fumbled with the lock while Grace began to dress, sitting on the floor, smiling. He finally managed to get the door open and fled.

'Don't worry,' he heard as he made off down the corridor. 'It's all right. Really.'

Liam sat at his desk and allowed his tears to flow gently; welling over the reddened line of his lower lids and down over his cheekbones until they ran into the dampening thatch of his beard and disappeared. Between the image of Grace's full, pale body, and the satisfaction of his own, came thoughts of Sophie, utterly loved and desired, betrayed by a passing moment of lust. This thought moved him very much until a picture of Grace, naked on the floor, arms open to him, thighs apart, floated into his mind, and Sophie, smiling and beautiful with the new baby on one hip, faded into the background and went out of focus. The two images see-sawed, each summoning their own intense and pleasurable feeling – now guilt: sharp and shocking; now desire: soft and irresistible.

Mo found him sobbing at his desk when she popped in at the end of the day. He looked up at her with no attempt to conceal his tears, and explained in a dull monotone what had happened. 'My God, Mo, what's happening to me?' he groaned as he finished. Mo stared at him in disbelief, then pushed her hair back over her high, shiny forehead.

'How could you?' she demanded harshly.

The humour briefly flickered again in Liam's eyes. 'It wasn't difficult. Not at the time.'

'Well, if it's just a joke . . .'

'No joke,' Liam sniffed. 'I know, how could I? But I did, and I couldn't help myself. I couldn't stop it. Mo, I adore Sophie, she's everything I could want – clever, funny, gentle.'

'So you just couldn't control yourself sexually?' Mo demanded furiously.

'Well, I suppose that's undeniable. But Sophie and I have a very good sex life. She's a wonderful lover. It's not that, even. There isn't any excuse. What shall I do?'

Mo shrugged crossly. 'What is there to do? It's done. I just can't understand why. You won't tell Sophie, will you?'

Liam shook his head.

'Well, you better pull yourself together before you go home. If Sophie sees you looking like that, you won't have to tell her.'

'Haven't you ever just wanted something, Mo?'

'Yes. But you don't have to take it, regardless of the consequences. . . .' Her voice faded a little towards the end of the sentence. 'The point is Sophie.' Her voice gaining certainty. 'Didn't you think about Sophie?'

'Yes, but it didn't have anything to do with wanting Grace. Specifically, wanting Grace's tits.'

'Can't you be serious?'

'I am serious. I seriously wanted those tits, and now I'm seriously sorry. And when I'm in bed with Sophie tonight, I'll seriously want her lovely slender body. It's all serious, Mo, but it's also difficult.'

'It makes no sense,' Mo said, as she fished into her shoulder bag and handed Liam some paper tissues.

'That's right, it makes no sense. Do you know what I really want? My most secret and compelling fantasy? When I'm lying in bed with Sophie asleep beside me, or when I sit here marking asinine essays, or, God help me, when I'm gazing down Grace's cleavage? I want to be a monk. Don't laugh. It's true. I imagine myself walking silent cloisters, my head bent in meditation, contemplating Creation. Or praying in my cell, searching quietly for the certainty of God. I wear a habit and my head is shaved into a tonsure. I don't even know if monks are like that any more. They probably wear Levi 501s and work for Greenpeace. The world isn't the way I would like it to be.'

'The world is the way you make it,' Mo said firmly.

Liam finished wiping his eyes. 'Are you quite sure of that?'

'Quite sure. Anyway, you'd make a dreadful monk, Liam.'

'You're probably right.'

'Why can't you just suffer and put up with it?'

'Like you do?' he asked, raising his thick eyebrows. 'What happened with your young existentialist? I've been watching you. Something happened, didn't it? There's been, I don't know, a change in you. An anger underneath all that sensibleness. You had an affair with him, didn't you?'

Mo sat very straight in her chair and took Liam's inquisitive gaze without flinching. She held herself taut and said coolly, 'No. Nothing happened.'

Liam raised his head in a slow nod of comprehension. 'Aah,' he smiled, 'so you nearly fell from grace too. And it hurts.'

'A rather poor joke, in the circumstances, even for you. I suppose I almost made a fool of myself. In any case, I don't have a Sophie in my life. It hurt for a moment, but it wasn't important.'

'Of course it hurt. It always hurts, and it goes on hurting. Let it hurt you, Mo. There are no wars to be won by pretending you're invulnerable. I'm afraid that unpleasant young man won't notice one way or another, but you should know what's happening to you.'

'Stop preaching at me Liam. You're the one I found crying. I almost got carried away one night, and there are no aftereffects.'

'Yes, my dear, you're right, I suppose. Perhaps I do envy you, after all.' He looked at his watch. 'It's time to go home,' he said quietly.

The end of term was also the end of Mo's direct dealings with Joe. She no longer had to watch his silent, superior smile during the weekly department meetings, or watch the girls she had seen at his side each week trying to achieve his indifferent expression, glancing sideways at him occasionally to see if they had got it quite right. Mo imagined him imparting his cynical wisdom to them, each one feeling set apart by their new view of the world, chosen as fit to break through the dull, conventional thinking to the bitter core of truth. Then, having been dropped from his programme, they were lost. Thrown by some new topic and unable to work out the correct position unaided, they fell back to the safety of the texts Mo had set, and reproduced what they read. Mo found satisfaction in this, and her capacity to hold on to a view of the world she knew to be right.

And although it was true that quite often, as she drove up to her house, she remembered how Joe had stood once at the top of the steps, waving his bottle of wine, it was no more than a picture, a memory. There was no pain attached. Her life was very much as it had been before the incident with Joe, quite full with work and occasional outings with Luke.

There was only one bad moment, the night after that evening with Joe. Luke had phoned to arrange a trip to the theatre. She was pleasant and enthusiastic. Yes, she was looking forward to it, why didn't they meet at such and such a place, and after the play go for a meal. But when they had put the phone down, she had wept, suddenly and very much to her surprise. As she splashed the tears away with cold water she admitted to herself that there must have been some fantasy, as she picked up the receiver, that it would be Joe wanting to see her again. Drying her face, she catologued Luke's qualities. He was straightforward and kind, talked interestingly about his work, asked intelligently about hers. And if he was a bit dull, she told herself sternly, so much the better, for life was about ordinary people getting on with ordinary things. About living in the real world, not the heroic, existentialist drama that Joe imagined, needing, as he did, a new excitement every day just to reassure himself that he was still alive. She would rather have solid Luke in her life.

After that she invited Luke around more frequently, and he was pleased since he enjoyed Mo's company, and there was never any problem with intensity. It occurred to him that Mo might eventually be the right person to settle down with, but he didn't mention it because things were all right as they were and, he thought, he would wait until she was back from her rainforest thing, and more settled.

Nine

Mo spent most of the Christmas vacation with Marjorie. Luke was going up north to see his family, and although Liam had invited her to spend Christmas with them, she felt uncomfortable about accepting under the circumstances. Joining in the family festivities, knowing what she knew about Liam, seemed a kind of treachery towards Sophie, as if *she* were somehow being unfaithful. Besides, Marjorie was alone and there was no question about where she ought to spend Christmas.

It snowed just after she arrived. Marjorie was delighted, and they donned wellingtons, gloves and scarves, and minted fresh impressions in the snow that covered the fields behind the back garden. 'As if,' Marjorie said, 'no one had ever set foot here before us.' Mo imagined their footprints disappearing with the next fall, or the first thaw, and the countless numbers of footfalls that had vanished, been wiped away by wind, rain and time. Centuries of time, deleting thousands of footprints. No one had left anything behind, or really made their mark lastingly on this landscape. A phrase came into her mind: 'a passing formulation of life.' She wondered where it was from.

They walked every day and sat each evening in front of the log fire, reading and smiling reassuringly at one another. It was not unpleasant. Even Marjorie's insistence on traditional Christmas day lunch – tough turkey, papery bread sauce, overcooked brussel sprouts – was funnier than it was grim. It was only Marjorie's reminiscences of John that caused Mo's fists to tighten, and that place in her diaphragm to contract. It began always with 'Do you remember . . . ?' as Marjorie attempted to recreate the time of 'the family', the three of them together, loving and laughing with each other. The anecdotes all had the same structure, similar to the burned cakes: some charming foolishness of Marjorie's that made the other two laugh and love her all the more. The Christmas when she had given everyone the wrong presents and John solemnly spent the day wearing a coral necklace while Mo puffed away on an empty Meerscham, and they speculated hilariously about what Granny and Grandpa would do with the glittery silver-lurex tights that had been destined for a particularly trend-setting cousin of Mo's. Mo listened and smiled, but wondered if, still, John would not rather have spent his Christmas with Sheila. If the moments of humour in their lives were not poor compensation for the grave and lasting mistake her father had made. And it occurred to her that there was perhaps something knowing about the way her mother's happiest memories depended on her giddiness. Did she sense that all that held them together was her helplessness – had she exploited that to keep John with her?

She smiled emptily at her mother's memories, but a rage began to build at the stupidity, the *lie* of it all. Mo thought furiously – what did *she* know about him. She didn't know him at all. Marjorie had no idea about the man she had been married to for nearly twenty years. She spoke of a myth, a fabrication, in complete ignorance of who he really was. His intelligence, his taste, his pleasures had been completely hidden from her. She spoke of a man who had cut away the best of himself in order to fulfil his duty to her. Her stories of his amusement described, in reality, only his patience and kindness and determination not to let his disappointment poison their lives.

Perhaps also, the thought began to insinuate itself, his cowardliness? Why, when he found Sheila, had he not grabbed his good fortune and run towards it? There would surely have been a way of remaining responsible for Marjorie without chaining himself to her. Perhaps Marjorie *had* offered something that Sheila could not. Was her father not strong enough to break away? To face a relationship with a woman who was his equal? Her suspicion that something like this might have been the case lurked in the anger she had felt during his last illness and after his death. The adult Mo had put it out of her mind. Now it came back, not with the furious, flashing moment of adolescent insight, but seeping, unwelcomed, into her vision of a tragic, thwarted and chivalrous man.

Mo did not notice, however, that integral to the fantasy of John and Sheila finding fulfilment with each other was the figure of Mo herself. The picture of the two of them making a life together contained Mo. She was part of the fantasy, not outside, viewing it as the child who had been left behind with Marjorie. It was the three of them, Sheila, John and Mo, who sat down to Provençal suppers, attended concerts, rambled in the Lake District. Mo remained ignorant of her presence in these dreams, and unaware that her presence was, indeed, the very essence of them.

There were times even, in dreams, when Sheila and Mo fused. Never having met her, Mo's dream-self imposed her own adult features on the unknown face of Sheila, so that essentially there were only two of them, John and Mo, living their charmed and civilized life. When she woke, the conscious Mo separated herself and Sheila out again so that she remembered only the two adults, neither of them her, along with some hazy, ill-defined other character misty in the background.

On the whole the vacation went quite smoothly. She enjoyed the peace and the walking, and had done a lot of reading by the first week of January: reports and papers on tropical rainforest ecosystems. The day before she was due to leave she received a card from Liam. The outside expressed a standard wish for peace and prosperity in the forthcoming year; inside was the devastating message that Liam had left Sophie and was now living with Grace. He asked Mo to meet him in the department two days before the beginning of term. Mo let out a cry as she read it.

'What's the matter, darling?' Marjorie asked, looking up from her morning paper.

'It's Liam. You remember, at college. He's leaving his wife.'

'Oh, dear,' her mother breathed gently.

'For a student.'

'Oh, dear.'

'He's got three children, one's a new baby. How can he be so irresponsible?' Mo exploded.

'I suppose he couldn't help himself,' Marjorie said sadly.

'For God's sake, Marjorie, you sound like Liam. You're not suggesting that that makes it all right?'

'No, darling. Of course it's not all right. But sometimes these things can't be helped. It's dreadful for the people who have been left behind, sometimes it's dreadful for the people who leave. But it happens anyway. You won't be unkind to him, will you? He probably needs your friendship.'

'Perhaps I should congratulate him?' Mo suggested swiftly.

'No, but it won't help if you make him feel worse than he does already.'

'You know nothing about it.'

Marjorie stirred her tea thoughtfully. 'No, I suppose not. Daddy never left me. But he had a friend, you know. A woman at the university.' She looked up to see Mo's shocked, pale face.

'You knew about it?'

'Yes. I heard them on the phone once. I never said anything, of course.'

'You knew it was going on all the time? Didn't you mind?'

'Well, at first I did. But then I wondered what I was minding about. You see, the three of us were very happy together, and I supposed that they, your father and the woman, were also happy. I think John needed both. I thought, why should I object to him being happy with someone else when it didn't affect us at all? So I let it be. He never wanted to leave. I knew he loved me. I wondered about the woman, sometimes. I think it must have been hardest for her. Especially when he died. I thought of inviting her to the funeral, but it didn't seem the right thing to do, and I didn't want to upset you more than you were already. But I was dreadfully sorry for her, shut out like that.'

Mo wanted to scream, 'What about me? What about me? I wasn't happy.' She felt outraged, betrayed. Their secret, John and Mo's, had been known all along. Their private world turned out never to have existed. She had only borne the knowledge of her father and Sheila loving each other by feeling included in the secret. Now Marjorie spoke of having protected her from knowing about Sheila. *Marjorie* protecting *her*! If everyone knew, then *she* was the fool. *She* was the outsider. And her mother talked about herself and John as if they were the central relationship, and she, Mo, hardly more than a bystander. It was unthinkable; had never been thought. It had not been like that, she told herself angrily, remembering the trust, the private looks that had passed between herself and her father. But now there was the possibility, from the easy, certain way her mother talked, that such unspoken glances had passed between the two of them, unnoticed by Mo.

It had never occurred to her before.

She remembered the anguish she had felt for her father, for his longing, for his loneliness. How she had tried, by loving him, to make up for that. He had tricked her. That was how she felt: that a cruel joke had been played on her.

'It wasn't like that,' she said harshly, glaring at Marjorie. 'You didn't understand.'

Marjorie looked at her daughter, flushed and tearful, like a small child.

'No, darling, perhaps not. I may not have understood. I expect I didn't. Let's forget it.'

Mo shot a look of venom at her mother as she got up from the table and ran upstairs to her bedroom.

'Oh, dear,' Marjorie thought to herself, as she stood up and began to clear the breakfast things from the table. 'If only Mo weren't so very convinced about everything.' She worried that Mo, so correct and right-thinking, would never see the small pleasures that life could offer; and that she would never find out that sometimes correctness had to be fudged a little to enable imperfect people to get on with their lives. It frightened her when she thought how few mistakes her daughter had made in her life. There had never been a moment when she had come to Marjorie for consolation for some small, ordinary foolishness, so Marjorie had not had the opportunity to tell her it didn't matter, that everyone made mistakes. It was rarely fatal, and was, in any case, useful when it came to dealing with the mistakes of others. Mo's inability to live with imperfection seemed to Marjorie much more dangerous than imperfection itself.

She wondered why Mo was like this and thought of John. Always calm and capable. He, of course, always tried to do the right thing. In his way. Perhaps he was too capable for Mo's good. Mo had never noticed the toll he'd had to pay for keeping everything going the way he did. And that others had to pay as well, perhaps.

And she herself 'managed' in her own way. It was so simple to let everyone else sort out the difficulties, and to keep the real difficulties to herself. She felt quite frightened for Mo and wished she could say something, but she did not know what.

She sighed and wiped her hands on the kitchen towel, leaving the breakfast things to drip-dry on the drainer, and got her book down from the mantlepiece. It was about tropical forests and how they were in danger of extinction. She had taken it out from the library last week, so that she could understand a little more about Mo's project. She settled herself in her chair by the fire and put on her reading glasses, before re-reading the sentence she had left off from the previous evening. It said that at the present rate of exploitation rainforests would be wiped off the face of the earth within twenty-five years.

Marjorie sighed again and put the book down on her lap. She would probably still be alive then. She did not know what to think about it. It seemed suddenly dreadful that within her lifetime something that existed since before mankind would not be there any more. But she was not sure why it was dreadful. She had not given rainforests a thought in her whole life until Mo was about to go to one. And it was probable that, already during her lifetime, several species of plant and animal had become extinct: been here and gone without her ever having been aware of them. But there was so much to think about once you started. So many things were at risk. One read and heard all the time of creatures and places and people that needed to be saved. What was one to do? And it all seemed so far away. Urgent, but remote. It was terribly hard to believe in the danger the world was in when she walked every day in the meadow and saw everything just as it always had been. She knew that she had been very privileged and cocooned from the nasty side of life – the meadow had always been there, it had all always been there. She felt troubled, but the enormity of it, once she started thinking, made her feel quite helpless. She could not see what she could do, about anything.

Marjorie closed the book and returned it to the mantlepiece. She decided to go to the shops and buy a cake for tea. It was Mo's last afternoon before going back to London, and she wanted it to be nice.

In the forest, four degrees above the equator, the temperature, season, and time of day dictated it time for the winged termites to swarm. They had been nurtured by worker termites for this moment when, released from their cells in the termitary, their silvered, sun-glinting wings carried males and females in a vast, sudden cloud on their single brief flight into the world.

A female dropped to the ground and waited. For death? For the return of her nurses to clean and feed her? For another glorious and unexpected winging through the bright air? She simply waited, bound by the necessity to wait that was built into her genes. Everything familiar was gone. Her world had been the termitary; everything that had been life, all she had known (in as much as knowing were possible to her) was finished. Waiting took its place. It was a death of sorts.

Sooner or later – and whether it was sooner or later meant nothing to a creature possessed of a brain too small to comprehend the passage of time – a winged male would glide down on the scent she unwittingly exuded. They would mate and, like a forever-innocent Adam and Eve, their opalescent wings would drop away, leaving them naked to crawl over the forest floor until a suitable place was found to lay her fertilized eggs. Now a queen, she would deposit eggs, generation after generation, until her offspring built the darkness back around her, and she was again enclosed within the termitary, and her world had been reborn.

Back in the south of England, Mo bade her mother a premature and cold farewell. She had decided to leave that evening, not wait for the following morning. Ignoring Marjorie's anxieties about driving back in the dark in such weather, she threw her suitcase into the back of her car and sped off as fast as the snowy road would permit. Once she was on the motorway she pressed down as hard as she dared on the accelerator, fairly flying along the fast lane in her need to get away from her childhood home. All that she remembered about the place she had grown up in, the quiet memories, intimacies, familiarities, were tainted now with what she perceived as treachery. There had been secrets; things had not been as she thought them to be. Her memories were no more than imaginings; wrenched away from her by the incompatible realities of others. Three individual sets of experience, the story of her life no longer the centre! There were three stories, not one. She felt cheated. They had stolen the world of her childhood. It turned out to have been no more than a piece in a jigsaw.

The forest, in the car heading for London, and in Borneo, was alert to a further shift of balance in the organism that was Mo. The loss of the growing place, it noted, did not come as it should to this creature, as unquestioned necessity, as a moment in the process of life, new-life and not-life. There was great disturbance at the heart of the system.

The part of the forest that was the new queen termite made itself known to Mo; shimmered the pattern of life and necessity at her.

But Mo, enveloped in rage, felt only the merest twinge of eternity, heard only the faintest echo of the forest. Neither was strong enough to distract her from the maelstrom of her anger. She confused the voice of the forest with the sound of the blood rushing through her veins, and the signal from the termite queen with her accelerated heart rate.

She pulled into a lay-by to give herself a chance to calm down. 'Pull yourself together,' she told herself, resting her head on the steering wheel and making herself breath slowly and regularly. Liam leaving Sophie, her mother's revelation that she had known all along the secret that was supposed to belong only to John and Mo, would not shake her. She would not permit either of those things, those *facts*, to stop her being what she was. She was not upset; just surprised, and that already was wearing off.

The forest faded back to the place in Mo that she did not know existed, as she felt her thudding heart slow down and the racing blood begin to flow more gently through her veins. That's better, she thought. She turned on the ignition and drove at her usual reasonable pace back to the city and her waiting flat.

Ten

Liam waited in the empty staff common room. Mo hadn't arrived, though it was half an hour later than the time he had suggested on his card. He sat broodily in an armchair wondering what it was he intended to say to Mo. Why indeed he intended to say anything. Perhaps she was the nearest thing he had to a confessor in his life. Why he didn't give up the struggle and join the Romans, he could not imagine. A bit too lush; too canny, they were. At least in the higher reaches of the organization, they understood, too well for Liam's taste, the complexities of human nature. Forgiveness was available for the mere expenditure of a few Hail Marys and contrition. He had to stick with the unforgiving Prots, who knew that sin was sin, that what was done could never be undone, and that everything had to be paid for forever.

Nothing less would do. The cold adjudicating eye of Anglican morality was what he wanted, because that in addition gave him something to fight. He wanted a good telling off, and then to rebel against the puritanical, death-loving, ungenerous creed that made life no more than something to be endured.

That was what he wanted Mo for. He was, after all, an avowed atheist, and could hardly go and beg the church's forgiveness when he loudly denied everything it stood for. Mo's secular severity would have to do. He knew that she would never understand what he had done, or why. She would accept no excuses; fallibility being not an excuse, but a fault. 'For my fault, for my fault, for my most grevious fault . . .' he intoned quietly. There I go again, he thought, the slightest lapse of concentration, and I'm a Catholic. A shudder passed through him, precisely balanced between terror and joy, as he thought of Grace, waiting for him in their new flat. My future, he muttered under his breath. I have Grace now, instead of God. Not a bad bargain, he supposed, in the short term.

Grace had arrived at his office the day after their first encounter. She sat patiently with her hands folded in her lap, smiling with a beatific confidence, as he explained, remotely and awkwardly, his eyes shifting between the papers on the desk and blinking incessantly, that he could not see her again. He apologized for having lost control; it should not have happened. It was entirely his fault, but he was, in fact, a happily married man with a family. He did not want to be unfaithful to his wife, whom he loved. They must both, he had told her gravely, put the previous day out of their minds.

Grace continued to sit and smile for several moments after he had finished. Long enough to allow Liam, dreamlike and disbelieving, to walk around his desk to where she sat and press his aching lips against her soft, smiling mouth, as his fingers undid the buttons of her silky acetate shirt. He took her lovely brown nipple into his mouth and sucked noisily on it, filling himself with her. She stroked his untidy hair, pushing him gently nearer to her, and as she moaned sweetly, 'Oh Liam, oh Liam, my darling. You're so wonderful,' he came like Niagara.

He explained again, afterwards, that he did not know what had come over him, and she left, still beaming a loving smile, saying that it was all right.

After several such scenes, Liam gave up the struggle for righteous behaviour. Instead of telling her that this must stop as she came through the door, he fell on her immediately, devouring her. They fucked like panthers; sweating, writhing, groaning. Twice, sometimes three times a day. As she walked into the room, her hands already undoing her clothes, he would jump up from his desk, lock the door, and feel the darkness of winter lift, as if his very own private sun had come to shine over him and chase the dullness from his soul.

When the term ended, they arranged to meet every day in his room in the department. Sophie suspected nothing; it was not unusual for Liam to go in to college during the vacation. His guilt at deceiving her was there, but so overlayed with lust for Grace that he barely noticed it. There was only a kind of dull surprise, as he left the house, that he should find it so easy to betray the only part of his life he cherished. He did not imagine for a moment that he had found something more valuable, not even in the sex, which was desperate and coarse compared to the delicate eroticism that had evolved between himself and Sophie. She was beautiful, even after three children; slim and exquisitely curved. Still a girl, at thirty-two, bright and lovely. He found her desirable, watching her at breakfast before going off to meet Grace, as she bustled about in one of his old shirts. He wanted her when he arrived home, exhausted from his exertions with Grace, as she kissed him and led him into the living room to sit and chat about their day.

But Grace's full, firm, nineteen-year-old breasts negated it all. Love, friendship, the children. Liam sat motionless in the common room aware of the terrible absurdity of it. How was it possible?

Before Christmas arrived he knew he could not live without Grace, that anything and everything would have to go before he could face life without her. Without her what? Not her brain, or her wit, or some deep underlying connection he felt with her soul. Her tits. He could not live without her tits. They were all of it: youth, promise, desire. Pushing their way through the world, full, ripe with life. It was their confidence, their absolute certainty that they were to be desired that spread over every inch of her, and made Liam incapable of doing anything but desire them. If he could not have God then he could have Grace's breasts, and it seemed to Liam that they alone filled the void. He implored her to live with him, and spoke of destiny when she mentioned his wife and family. Finally she agreed, because she did love and admire him, as well as feel flattered and excited by his need for her. He would be lover and father to her and could teach her so much about life. She was sorry about his family, but knew these things happened, her own parents had met, after all, while married to other people. It could not be helped. Liam took care of telling those who had to be told; her parents, his wife; and survived their shock and distress through the busyness of moving out and finding a place for them to live. Sophie's anger and sorrow nearly broke his heart. And the children . . . But by New Year he and Grace had moved in together.

He knew he was going to live with a stranger, that the losses would be enormous. The whole enterprise was laden with doom. It was a ticket on the *Titanic*. There could only be a single outcome. Having wiped out everything except his sense of despair, he felt a grim satisfaction that now, at last, he was committed to it. The price to be paid for despair is despair, and there was, at least, something clear about it.

He sat on in the armchair, miserable and contented, as the door opened and Mo walked in carrying a pile of books. She nodded seriously to Liam.

'I wasn't going to come, but I had to bring some books back to the library.' She looked almost ill, her face pale and drawn above her cream turtle-necked sweater. There were purple shadows under her eyes, and her hair fell lank around her shoulders. She put the books on a table and pushed her hair back over her forehead with both hands.

'You don't look well. You should have stayed in bed.'

'I'm fine. I wasn't going to come because I didn't want to talk about your little drama.' She sat down heavily in a chair and sighed. 'Oh, Liam, how can you be so silly – so predictable?'

'Mmm . . .' Liam rested his elbows on the arm of the chair. 'It's funny, but it doesn't feel predictable when you're the one who's doing it. It feels like my own, private, unique life happening. I may be just a statistic about middle-aged men, but to Sophie and the kids, and me, and possibly Grace, it feels like real life. Until it happened, I couldn't have done it, then I couldn't not do it.'

Mo shook her head stubbornly. 'You elevate it into a Greek tragedy, but it isn't. You didn't have to leave Sophie for some passing sexual need.'

'Perhaps there's more to sexual need than sexual need,' Liam murmured mournfully.

'Rubbish. You're destroying people's lives for nothing. For *nothing*.'

Liam blinked his eyes and kept them shut momentarily.

'Yes, you're right. I know how slight it is compared to Sophie and the children, but even knowing that all along, I did it. Let's not discuss it, Mo. I just wanted to let you know what had happened. Sophie's terribly upset, of course. She's gone with the children to her brother in Devon for a few weeks. Grace and I have rented a flat in Willesden. She won't be back as a student next term – I don't think that matters very much. And I'm thinking of resigning. We may go to Zambia, there's a job for me at the university in Lusaka if I want it. We'll see.'

'Liam, you're mad.' Mo was aghast at the finality, the cutting away of any route back.

He smiled painfully. 'You're right, my dear, as ever. I didn't forsee a very comfortable old age for myself – to say nothing of eternity. Never mind, it can't be helped.'

Mo almost shouted at him, 'It can be helped. You can stop it now.'

Liam smiled again and shook his head. 'The bridges are all burnt, my dear. Grace and I are going to have to swim for it, I'm afraid.'

Mo got through the next two weeks on routine, hardly aware of its passing. She drove every day from Kentish Town to Bloomsbury, beginning to notice how oppressive the university buildings were. The grey stone structures that housed libraries, laboratories, lecture theatres, seemed to loom, too monumental for the people who bustled in and out of them. Individuals passing through the great stone entrances appeared to be swallowed up, insignificant morsels, like plankton disappearing into the gaping mouth of a great whale. There was something dreadfully gloomy about the whole area that had once seemed to Mo to possess a glow of learning and tradition. Now it weighed down on her.

There was very little in her life that felt pleasurable. She taught her course for that term more or less automatically, then returned home and made herself something convenient to eat. In the evening she worked, marking essays, setting exam papers for the following term; listened to the news on the radio; bathed and went to bed. She saw Luke with as little pleasure as she went to work, as more of an obligation than anything. And when they slept together it was the same.

Mo knew herself to be in a dull condition, and she was aware that she was angry with people: with Liam and her mother. But it was a dull anger, more of an impatience with their foolishness, a nuisance that they had rocked the boat. She spoke to Liam when they met on the stairs in the department, or in the common room. But the old familiarity had gone. She no longer popped into his room for coffee, nor did she invite him to hers. She thought he looked miserable and exhausted, but then so he should, he could hardly blame anyone but himself. He gave her, when they met, affectionate smiles and asked with real concern how she was. As if he were worried about her health. She always wanted to say that it was himself he should be worried about, but in fact replied that she was fine, not unpleasantly, but nor in a manner that offered further conversation. He would nod sorrowfully and go on his way.

She did not see Joe at all. His courses had not begun yet. It was as if he weren't there, and she hardly thought about him. Sometimes that picture of him standing by her chair, making his offer, flashed unexpectedly into her mind, but it was always accompanied by her dismissal of him as contemptible and callow. Sometimes, when she thought of Liam, she found herself picturing her father and, once or twice, Joe, and was surprised by the confusion of images in her mind. She allowed that there was something about her father not leaving her mother, and Liam deserting Sophie, that had connected in her. But, she insisted to herself, they were in fact quite different situations, and because minds play tricks on their owners didn't mean the tricks were true or useful. She wondered a lot about her mother, knowing all those years about Sheila. When she sat at home, reading *Nature* or *Scientific American*, her mind would wander back to Marjorie. Once she had got over the initial shock, what was extraordinary was that Marjorie, of all people, should have known all along, and kept it quietly to herself. And she had spoken so calmly about it, as if, all the while, she had been trying to protect Mo. That was not how things had been at all. It was not, Mo was certain.

She began to find it all – everything – faintly disgusting, as if she had a permanently bad taste in her mouth. She lived through her final two weeks in England with a baleful vision that encompassed everything around her. When she shopped, she wandered around the supermarket filled with the produce of the world; basic necessities, exotic treats. She found nothing she wanted to eat, and arrived at the check-out with an almost empty basket. She bought frozen smoked haddock and a cube of frozen leaf spinach which was not unpleasant and needed no effort. But essentially it was people who distressed her. Everywhere, in all circumstances, she found the human race distasteful. They spilled untidily on to the streets, going about their business, talking, forever talking, about nothing. Words seemed to issue forth from humanity like overflowing garbage. Lords of the universe, kicked into supremacy by the acquisition of language, they talked and talked. But about what? What was this extraordinary development used for? Who had anything to say? One afternoon she went to Selfridges to buy a clock for her trip. On the way to the lift she overheard a middle-aged woman explaining to her husband at the lighter counter, 'I don't care how good they are, I don't want one of those flip-top things. They aren't ladylike.' Mo's pale face blazed scarlet as she turned and stared at the woman. Dowdy, respectable, lips pursed, cheeks cracked with face powder; designed entirely from head to toe to fit in with her neighbours, she was of no obvious interest to anyone except her husband. For a second Mo was filled with a flaring hatred for the nondescript woman, and fought down an urgent need to take her by her scrawny neck and squeeze the life out of her. If she had allowed any sound to pass the barrier of her clenched teeth, she would have screamed: 'You stupid, stupid cow. What's the point of you? Did the human race spend millions of years struggling to its feet, learning, discovering, surviving against all the odds, so that you could stand here now, pursing your fastidious lips and drivelling on about being ladylike?'

The venom she felt took Mo by surprise. She thought, this isn't me. This is more like Joe's vision of the world. Perhaps I'm ill. It's unreasonable to be so angry about nothing. But sitting over a coffee upstairs, she realized that, to a less violent extent, this was how she had been feeling about people for some time. Disgust simmered inside her. She looked about and saw food disappearing into open mouths, and then imagined those who had been filling their bodies, naked, washing, soaping, cutting toenails. She saw millions of tiny little lives; short, pointless existences. Fatuous individuals, fussing over social niceties, washing their net curtains, clipping their hedges, gossiping to one another about those who had slipped up, were not quite up to scratch, according to the rules. Each of them sitting there, sipping and wiping the corners of their mouths, concealing the evidence that they were contained in bodies that had normal, biological requirements; thinking that it mattered, that they mattered. How did all that fit in with the nobility of the human race, the immortality of the soul, the endless pages of print from scientists, philosophers and poets? Primitive man or twentieth-century surburban man – what salvation, what damnation, what soul? Rubbish. Rubbish. It was all rubbish. Self-deceiving claptrap to prevent us from seeing our own insignificance. These people ate, shat, and procreated – and lived too long, so there was nothing left for them to do once they had outlived their biological usefulness but sit around in cafés in department stores and stuff their faces, and talk, talk, talk. Stupid, ignorant and unnecessary.

The forest had no opinion about the stupidity or ignorance of the elements that made it up. It existed simply through the existence of those elements and that was all the necessity there was. There were no destinies in the forest, just individual systems which were themselves comprised of smaller elements. They had only to function: molecules to attach themselves correctly to other molecules, DNA chains to encode accurately enough to switch on and off the required chemical processes, leaves to transpire, flowers to fertilize, insects, birds and mammals to survive long enough to reproduce themselves so that the food chain might be maintained. To eat, be eaten, and decay. For none of these aspects was destiny-relevant, only what is, while it is. If an outsider concluded that the destiny or purpose of the parts of the forest *was* the forest, they would be wrong, for the forest itself was nothing more than the multitude of its parts, not above them, or subsuming them. The forest could not look on any part with contempt, for the disgust it felt would be for itself. But the forest, of course, did not feel anything, and was unable therefore to relate the turmoil in Mo to anything recognizable in its millions of years of existence. It could do no more with it than consign it to the category 'disturbance' once again.

A virus, the doctor said, and Mo was quite relieved to hear it. Probably mononucleosis, but it wasn't worth doing a complicated blood test since they couldn't do anything about it anyway. Lots of rest, and facing the fact that she would feel tired and depressed until it had worked its way out of her system.

Of course, Mo knew perfectly well that the mononucleosis virus was present in the air all the time. She taught, after all, a course on the history of disease. Mononucleosis had once, in the human race's more primitive state, been endemic. Everyone had it by the time they were five or six, and no one was any the worse for it. It was so common that it was virtually without symptoms. (That was true, too, of syphilis once.) But with the coming of clothing and separate accommodation; the coming, that is, of civilization, the pathogens had mutated and humanity lost its resistance. They contracted the viruses more rarely, but they felt worse once they had them. Now mononucleosis was known as the 'kissing disease', (and syphilis was venereal) since sexual contact was about the only close physical contact there was. But still, like the influenza virus, they were around all the time, and only some people contracted the diseases. What remained a mystery was who fell ill and when and why. And doctors said, 'Well, you have a virus . . .' meaning, 'You're not well, but we can't do anything about it.' It seemed that getting ill was the result of not being very well in the first place. As far as viral illnesses were concerned we weren't much further than magic.

Nonetheless, Mo felt better having had a diagnosis, and spent the last week in bed resting. By the time her departure date came she was beginning to feel more like herself again and the trip to the rainforest seemed to her, after Joe, Liam, her mother, and being ill, like a pot of gold at the end of the rainbow. A clearing away of the emotional confusion that others were pouring all over her.

Eleven

Nick came round last night, late, after I'd gone to bed. Apart from the hour, one look at him as I opened the door told me something was wrong. He obviously hadn't slept for days, his eyes had that burned, exhausted, desperately awake look of someone who had gone so long without sleep that they fear they have lost the capacity forever. Haunted but exultant. His fingers combed his blond curls obsessively, front to back, again and again. As soon as he saw me in the doorway he began.

'I must talk to you, Mo. Let's have a coffee.' He walked past me and sat at the table. I put some water on to boil and then sat opposite him in my nightdress and dressing gown.

'Nick, it's late and I'm tired. Couldn't it wait?'

'No, no, it can't wait.' The urgency in his voice was more than just the excitement I had heard before when he wanted to talk about some discovery he had made. It was as if he had a time limit, that what had to be told had to be told before it was too late. As if time (or he?) were running out. The words tumbled through his tense, thin lips, racing to get said.

'In quantum theory,' he began as if in the middle of a conversation, 'once two particles have interacted they become part of one physical system. You can never again describe them individually. See? Even when they've separated, it doesn't matter how far apart they get, you still can't know what one is doing without taking the other into account. They affect each other forever, Mo. You can't make any assessment of the likely behaviour of one without including information about the other. It *all* has to be known.'

I stared at him, feeling very tired, and increasingly uneasy.

'So what, Nick?'

'Interaction happens at every level, from individual particles colliding, to us functioning in the world as groups. Do you see? Even when we do an experiment – when we look at anything – there's an interaction between the looker and what he's looking at. Forever. So it's all connected. *We* are all forever connected with everything. There are no accidents. We are affected by *it*, so is our history, our whole development as a species. That's a universal force, not an accident. Everything we do is *influenced*.'

He emphasized this last word by drawing it out, and leaning across the table to stare intently at me. I became alarmed, the word, and the way he used it, spoke not of scientific insights but of psychotic delusion.

'Nick,' I said carefully, 'you can't take an abstract theory in modern physics and use it to prove intention in the universe. You're talking about two completely separate levels of reality. Particles aren't complex human beings. *They* may be influenced, but they don't have brains, logic. They don't think.'

'Assumption.' Nick dismissed my argument. 'Separation. That's what we do all the time so we don't have to see the truth. People have known this for millennia, but they were scorned as mystics. Now science itself is discovering those truths and they're right in front of our noses, in the language we like best. And what do we do? We separate everything: humans in this box, the physical world in another, and religion somewhere else. Then we feel safe again. But it's all connected. We are matter, and we have to abide by universal laws, just like anything else. We are part of a process, a plan.'

While he talked his hands were never still, they stroked, combed or rubbed his face and hair, or performed a staccato dance on the table, beating out a rhythm that might have been to a code to anyone able to interpret it.

'You're confusing different things,' I insisted. 'Physics is about things, not people. You're getting yourself terribly worked up.'

Nick glared at me. His face was flushed, as if he had a fever. Two red spots flared at the top of his cheekbones, and his eyes were damp and shining with excitement.

'Wrong. Wrong. Wrong,' he chanted. 'Modern physics is a signal to us, a sign. The human race is evolving to a new spirituality, in spite of itself. We think we're moving in the opposite direction, that science and technology are materialist developments. Not at all. Not at all. We deceive ourselves, Mo. We are taking a rational route to God. That's our way.' He banged the table with his fist. 'The computer is just our current attempt to create God. Technological progress isn't away from God, but towards him. What else is it but an attempt to define and create an intelligence beyond our own? What's that if not God, tell me that? Darwin, evolution; space travel, artificial intelligence: they're part of a pattern. Our progress to God. We just think we're going the opposite way. Do you understand?'

'No,' I snapped. I found myself getting angry, in spite of my increasing anxiety for Nick. He ignored me and continued with mounting enthusiasm.

'Technology appears to be mechanistic. It isn't. It's our method of meditating. Our brains aren't equipped to imagine what is alien, so, without even knowing what we're really doing, we create a form of intelligence that *can* comprehend the incomprehensible for us.' Here he laughed gleefully, and then lowered his voice conspiritorially. 'We are inventing God, you see,' he beamed at me. 'And when we've got it right, God will exist – as He has existed since before time, before humanity, before God himself. God invented God. Now *we* must invent Him to prove to Him that He's been here all along.'

He sat back, triumphant, and seemed to relax a little. He had made his case and was satisfied with it. But it seemed to me that behind the bizarre philosophy and the glee lurked a knowledge that he was slipping into madness. A terror flickered behind the wide, blue eyes, that knew he was moving outside the bounds of what society found acceptable, and more than that, what he found acceptable. Just as Nick wanted to look normal in his dress but couldn't, so his eyes flashed the pain of knowing his mind was not functioning as it should. He knew he was in danger. Behind the words and logic was a visible plea for help. 'Will you help me buy a proper jacket, Mo?' he had asked so often, knowing we would never accomplish the feat.

I wanted to talk to that part of him directly; to address the pain I saw in his eyes, but I knew that words would not work. He was going mad with words. Language would be the vehicle of his insanity, the means by which the tangle in his mind would try to unravel itself into the outside world. I might receive his messages of anguish, but I couldn't find a way to talk to it directly. I didn't know the language any more.

And I was scared for myself.

I had seen my own eyes in the mirror when I was . . . not myself. I take care these days when looking into mirrors, especially when the mirrors are other people's eyes.

'The pain,' Nick said suddenly, as though picking up the direction of my thoughts. 'The pain of sensing *more*, that there is more, of being half-way to the universal spirit. The pain of sensing God, but being unable to grasp Him because our brains just aren't wired for it. We'll do it in the end, but in the meantime, there's the terrible pain of reaching out.' His arm extended to perform the action, stretching up and out in front of him, then pulling back until his closed fist was a couple of inches in front of his face. He gazed at it for a moment, and opened his hand slowly to stare into his empty palm, stunned, like a child tricked into believing it would inevitably contain a coin.

'Nick,' I tried. 'Listen to me. You're not well. I think you may be ill. Why not get into bed? We can talk in the morning. I think you need to get some sleep.'

He continued to stare at his open palm for a second or two, as if he hadn't heard me. Then he looked up and grinned suddenly, reciting:

> Eeny, meeny, miny, mo
> Catch a quantum by the toe,
> Once you've got it, it won't let go,
> Eeny, meeny, miny . . . MO!'

I couldn't persuade him to stay. But I must admit some relief as the door closed behind him. I knew he was in a bad way, and of course I was worried, but I couldn't see what I could do to help. It's true that I didn't want disturbance in my life, and Nick's ramblings seemed to seep into my orderly routine, threatening to break it apart. It wasn't what he said, that was confused nonsense. It was the imposition of his needs that frightened me. As I offered him my bed I resented having to do so, and saw what I wanted slipping away: to sleep, to wake, to do the work scheduled for the day. Nothing else, nothing that demanded I stop and deal with the unexpected. This sounds callous. Had Nick said he wanted to stay the night, meaning he wanted my attention, to be cared for, I would have made him welcome and done whatever it seemed he needed. But I didn't want to; deep inside me his distress was an unwelcome intrusion. If that is callous, then that's what I am. I can offer him a friendship in his tentative sanity; I can do nothing for his madness. I'm not equipped. I do only what I can do.

In any case, it was clear by this morning that he was far beyond any help I could give him. I got a call at eight asking if I knew someone called Nick. He had been found some hours before by a passing patrol car, with hammer and tin-tacks, posting numerous sheets of scrawled-on paper up on the imposing doors of the Science Museum in South Kensington. He was wearing, apparently, striped pyjamas, carpet slippers and a yellow kagoul. The police hauled him into the car, but before they reached the station to charge him with a breach of the peace and damaging public property, they realized, from his wild explanations about quantum mechanics, Darwin, God and the relationship between being and becoming, what they had on their hands, and changed course for the nearest emergency psychiatric unit.

So they told me on the phone.

They found no identification on him, but my phone number was gleaned from the equation:

$$\frac{415\,2664}{\text{MO}} \times \frac{\text{OLD NICK}}{666} = \tfrac{1}{2}\,(\text{CHAOS} \times \text{MADNESS})$$

It continued: HELPHELPHELPHELPHELP . . . until the end of the page.

I called Carolyn Roberts before she left for work and told her that I would be in late today, not that it mattered really, since the flat would be clean and empty long before she returned home, but I wanted to be sure she had no plans to leave the gallery early. She said, a little puzzled, that it was fine, but that if there was a problem, not to bother coming this week. I assured her I'd be there and that the flat would be attended to. It was part of my routine; I would allow it, if necessary, to be disturbed, but not altogether disrupted.

'Well, if you're sure . . .' she said doubtfully, in her throaty, melodic voice. It was, it occurred to me, the first time we had spoken since the day I took the job. Until today we had communicated only by notes left on the kitchen table, rarely mine – the odd reminder to get more wax polish, or replace the leather for cleaning the glass. Her messages were more regular: a monthly cheque with a note saying something like, 'Wonderful . . . you are marvellous. Thanks so much. Love Carolyn.'

Of course, I was upset and worried about Nick, but that was all the more reason to try and continue with things as normally as possible.

Nick sat in a side room off the psychiatric admissions ward, wearing clean hospital pyjamas and a striped towelling dressing gown, open because they had taken away the belt. He barely looked at me as I entered the room. His eyes roved the walls and ceiling as if trying to catch something that was continually ducking out of his line of vision. When he spoke his voice had a peculiar, unfamiliar quality about it: pitched an octave too high, breathless and unnaturally jovial, as if he felt he were being overheard and had to conceal the urgency of his words with an asinine English-gent tone of voice.

'I'll leave you then,' the charge nurse nodded to me. 'I'll have to lock the door, I'm afraid, but there's a bell if you want me.' He pointed to a small button beside the bed Nick sat on.

'Oh, yes. Yes, yes, good. Fine. Yes, we're fine, thank you. Thank you so much.' Nick twittered, a smile as to an idiot on his face. When the charge nurse had left and the key turned in the lock, Nick's smile dropped away. He beckoned me to sit next to him on the bed; closer, closer still, and lowered his voice to a conspiratorial hiss. 'Mo,' he whispered, 'they're listening. Keep your voice down.'

I said, 'It's all right, Nick. Don't worry.' Trying to soothe the anxiety. It was dreadful to see him like this, even if not entirely unexpected. It hadn't happened for a long time, not since he was discharged the last time. I wasn't shocked or frightened, I'd seen this before several times when I was in hospital. But I hated being brought back to all that. I had hoped not to find myself in a place like this again, and it was very hard for me to walk through the swing doors of the ward this morning. I had armoured myself against it, and kept telling myself I was there as a visitor. But the sight and smell of the place hit me immediately and I had to stand for a moment to stop myself from turning tail and running as fast as I could away from there.

There is a strange silence about psychiatric wards, none of the clatter and bustle of ordinary medical business going on. You don't see nurses marching efficiently and noisily about, plumping pillows, popping thermometers into mouths, changing bedpans. You don't hear the chirpy inconsequentialities they offer as they pass beds. 'Hello, Mrs Jones, feeling all right today, are we?' Instead the nurses walk swiftly but silently on their heels to points of crisis, like ghosts gliding to a haunting. And apart from those moments of crisis, the silence pierced with human cries, there appears to be nothing going on at all. A nurse may be sitting on someone's bed, or beside someone's chair, just chatting, all her jobs for the day apparently over and with nothing else to do. It wouldn't occur to you, as an innocent onlooker, that just chatting was the main and most difficult part of her tasks for the day. Or his. Psychiatric wards are to be distinguished by the high number of men in white nursing coats. It's like a place in permanent hiatus, a corridor of life, and the skills are those of waiting and containment. The patients, too, seem to wait.

They wander in ones and twos, in slippers and dressing gowns, able-bodied if hypnotically slow, as if they had some dreadful disease diagnosed and were waiting for it to strike.

It all came back to me so powerfully, as I stood this morning in the doorway, trying not to run away. The incongruous, drugged calm; the sudden flurry of activity when someone broke through the pharmacological barrier back to madness and noise. It wasn't that I had forgotten and now remembered: I hadn't known I'd noticed.

'They've taken all my notes away,' Nick was saying. 'But it doesn't matter, I've got it all in my head.'

Nick was high and crazy. They were giving him no medication until the ward doctor had done his round later in the morning, and he was racing with madness. But much of what he said was coherent enough, at least in terms of his normal thought patterns; a repetition of his researches. It was a matter, really, of lifting the coherent phrases from the surrounding babble. He seemed to be encoding his speech, inserting between the sense what information theorists call redundancy, or 'noise'. Into the unfamiliar but understandable things he had to say he interposed a frenzied jabbering – snippets of advertising jingles, irrelevant proverbs, old songs – all offered in a tone of voice that suggested immense significance. His tone implied that these impenetrable phrases were the import of what he had to say. The parts of his speech that I could make sense of were spoken in an offhand, inattentive way, as though they had unaccountably slipped in and counted for nothing. I couldn't make out if this were deliberate, to throw 'them' off the scent, or if he were actually unable to assess what was meaningful. In addition to this there was a second conversation going on that I heard only half of – his replies to an unseen other in the room who seemed to demand his thought and attention from time to time, so that he would become momentarily abstracted and concentrated, nod or shake his head vigorously, and finally respond with an impatient, 'Yes, yes, I know *that*!' or 'That's not true!' to the – to me – soundless interruption. Then he would turn back to me as if nothing had happened, or rather, as if I should think that nothing had happened, and resume his monologue. He spoke for an hour at high speed, his hands all the while living a life of their own, his fingers weaving patterns around each other, and his eyes continuing to roam the high corners of the room. I was not required to respond to what he said, only to listen and to be seen to be listening. Every now and again he would glance at me sharply, dragging his eyes from their own special business of restless wandering and searching, to check that he had my attention. If I failed to nod in what were to him appropriate places, or appeared to lose concentration, he would stop and say briskly, 'Mo, are you getting this? Pay attention.'

I tried.

He told me, between his interruptions, more or less what he had said the night before, but when he had explained about our evolutionary progress to a higher intelligence via technology, his face suddenly froze into a bright, public grin. 'This message comes to you through the miracle of public service satellite.' He hummed a brief anthem, and then the frozen smile of the TV personality disappeared and a look of terror came over his face as he whispered, 'I'm a channel, Mo. I'm the final link in a vast chain of communication. They are using me, using me . . .' He looked anguished, and his hands flew to his face to cover the pain. 'I've been watched all along. The Book wasn't mine, it was theirs. They seeded me. Influenced what I read and when I was fully programmed, they switched on the satellite and linked me with all the computers in the world. The message is coming through me, there is a final concentration of energy. Through me.'

I reached out to take his hand, but he snapped out of that and returned to his previous explanations. When he finished I tried to talk to him, to suggest that he wasn't well, that he needed help. But he only stared at me for a moment and then turned his face away and began to talk to the other one in the room. Suddenly I wasn't there any more. I didn't exist. He complained loudly to whoever he was addressing, in the voice of an aggrieved child, about the unfairness of having been chosen to project the message.

'It's all very well for you, sir,' he snapped crossly, 'but I'm the one that has to do the dirty work.' He listened. 'Well, I can't. I can't. Get someone else. You do it if you're so fucking omnipotent. They won't listen to me, you know. All right. All right, I'm sorry . . . but it's very difficult, very difficult . . .'

His lower lip pouted and began to tremble as he rubbed one side of his face and tried to sniff back the tears bravely. 'I don't like it here,' he wept, turning to me again. 'Take me home. I want to go home.'

There wasn't anything I could do to help him. I pressed the bell and said to the charge nurse that I would be back to see him tomorrow. I left with the charge nurse sitting on his bed, trying to talk Nick down. 'It's all right. Don't be upset. The doctor will be here soon and you'll feel better.'

I got to Regent's Park Road by midday and let myself into Carolyn's ground-floor flat. The house is opposite Primrose Hill, and sometimes from the front room you can hear the sounds of the zoo. In particular, the monkey houses. Not often; usually there is just the sound of traffic and the hum of the central heating boiler, but occasionally there's a rising cry that disturbs the sound of the city. And disturbs me too. It always takes me by surprise, finding myself for a second somewhere else. In the wrong place. It doesn't last for long before I remember that the zoo is as much a part of the city as the buses and paving stones.

Carolyn runs an art gallery and the walls of the spacious front room are covered with paintings by her artists, brought here because they give her particular pleasure. I imagine that is why she bought the flat in the first place, for the space the walls provide. It is a vast, elegant house, built for the gracious living of a large and well-supported Edwardian family. Even divided into several flats, the sense of space remains. What were once servants' quarters at the top of the house provide accommodation for two contemporary families. Carolyn's flat takes up the entire ground floor. The front room is enormous and very grand. High ceilings with latticed mouldings designed to complement a weighty and impressive chandelier; white walls, one long and unbroken, another framing a deep, tiled fireplace that gives the room its human direction; and the bay window. Running from floor to ceiling and almost the width of the house, its gleaming expanse of glass is uncurtained, compelling passers-by to turn their heads and gaze as if at a shop window and rewarding them with a glimpse of the framed abstract shapes and colour that hang on the wall opposite. The light pours in as if to spotlight the paintings on the back wall, dust motes dancing in the beams. And from inside, looking out, there is the theatre of Primrose Hill: dogs freed from their leashes, children stamping up then racing down the incline, joggers looking heroic from a distance, old people struggling as far as they can before the hill defeats them to a thoughtfully placed bench, where they feed the birds from plastic carrier bags, or just sit and watch, as I do for a moment on entering that room, the world as it passes by.

But for all its theatricality, it's a comfortable room. There is a soft, cavernous old sofa, covered in rich brown velvet, and, facing the fireplace, two comfortable armchairs, bought as junk and carefully renovated by Carolyn's tasteful, talented hands. It is a room for friends to gather and relax in. I imagine the evenings, the fire lit, people sunk into the sofa, sipping wine and chatting easily to one another as Carolyn busies herself in the rambling kitchen across the hall, laying the oak refectory table with charming china and pretty glasses. The flat is centred around friendship, and the enjoyment of objects made with skill and care for use by those who can take pleasure in handling such things. And again in the kitchen, opposite the wide, oak dresser, the ceiling-high windows, looking out, here, on to a careless but attended garden that seems to wait for sun and friends to carry out glasses and food, and to spread rugs, delighted to take the opportunity for lunch outside.

This is the most comfortable house I see during the week. And complete in the sense that it stems from Carolyn herself. It is not, like the others, designed, but seems to have come together through the character of Carolyn. Actually, of course, nothing is accidental; everything has been thought about and arranged with care.

I clean this place gently. Bringing out its nature requires scented waxes and soft cloths. The wood is to be fed and nourished, not just dusted and polished like other places, and I apply the wax with gentle, circular motions, emphasizing the grain of the wood, feeling it absorb the nourishment as a plant absorbs sunlight. And with equal care I polish the floors and wipe over the skirtings. At last I renew the garden flowers with whatever is available outside, and place them in their small ceramic jug in the centre of the table. It is not a question of meticulous cleaning, of eradicating dust and dirt, but of giving attention. When I have finished the flat is right again, like the others on my schedule, but here the process seems to me different. It is the act of caring for the place, not the resulting lack of dust, that achieves the end. The flat glows when I've done, like a child who's been told it is clever and beautiful, and it's ready to be lived in with pleasure and comfort by those who can simply enjoy it.

Today, when I had finished, I made myself a cup of tea and sat drinking it on the sofa. This isn't usual for me. Carolyn's notes often invite me to help myself to tea or coffee, to eat her biscuits or sample leftovers in the fridge from a dinner party the night before. I never do. I finish the work, then spend a few moments walking through the flat looking at it, enjoying the results of my work. To eat or drink or sit would be to use the place, and that is not what I want to do. But today was different, I felt somehow that I had the right, or perhaps the need, to benefit from my efforts. Or it may have been simply that I'd had nothing to eat or drink all day, and after the distress of last night and this morning, just wanted to sit quietly for a little while in congenial surroundings. I sank into the velvet cushions and sipped my tea from a pretty china cup garlanded with cottage flowers and felt better. I had soothed away most of the disturbance of Nick's breakdown, gaining, I think as much from the attention I gave to the flat as it had. I felt that everything was back in place inside me, that my internal order had been re-established. I had felt,

I realized, in danger in the hospital, listening to Nick's confusions, and recognized the tiny shifts in the boundaries of my own order, as if my own pattern were shaken and under threat. Now I felt peaceful again, myself. I didn't think about Nick, about whom I can do nothing, but remembered the dream I'd had, after he left. A forest dream again, but this time I was above it, not in it.

I was standing on a mountain peak, precipitously high, looking down on the endless canopy of the rainforest. A mass of green reached out below me to the horizon, millions of tree tops that completely concealed what lay beneath. I knew the forest existed under the layers of foliage, but there was only the continuous green covering as far as the eye could see. A carpet, or a cloud, that blocked out the earth. Then, as if I were looking through binoculars, I found my vision focusing in closer, seeing the canopy through a greater magnification, although all the time I remained standing on the mountain staring down. At first I saw nothing different, then the individual leaves became apparent, and the continuous, flat greenness was broken up into millions of leaves of differing shapes and shades, moving slightly, jerking this way and that in the air currents two hundred feet above ground. I seemed to see each leaf's edge, sharply defined, separate from the rest as the continuity was broken up by the millions of discrete shapes and outlines that danced and glistened in the sun. Then closer, and the central veins and tributaries of the leaves became apparent, further destroying the unity, so that even the leaves were no longer simple single shapes. And then, unwillingly, closer still, to outlined cells, then molecules, then infinitely small particles dancing and leaping about their nuclei. The canopy was a mass of writhing movement, no longer anything solid or unified but minute pinpoints of matter, whirling, leaping, colliding without sense or order. I watched this, horrified; appalled by it. There was nowhere to go. I would not descend the mountain into that turmoil, to go into it would be to become part of it. Nothing would make me do that. And then suddenly Nick was there beside me, sitting at my feet, his knees drawn up to his chin, looking down, as I was, on the dreadful landscape.

'Beautiful, isn't it?' he murmured dreamily, and looked up at me with laughing excited eyes. 'That's how it is with everything, you know. All that mess and movement making order. Quite accidently.'

I put my arms around myself, hugging the upper part of my body tightly.

'No. That's how things are with you. I won't have it,' I said.

'You can't help it,' he smiled. 'You're it too. Look . . .'

And I knew what he wanted me to look at, and what I would see when I turned my gaze from the forest canopy first to him and then on myself. I would not; I was going to keep my eyes fixed on the chaos below, to keep from seeing something far worse, much more terrible. But the pressure of maintaining the direction became too great and I felt the muscles around my eyes pulling away, despite my efforts to prevent them moving.

I woke in a sweat of terror before I had seen what I so badly didn't want to see, and lay awake in the darkness of my room shivering and fearful and longing for daylight.

I sat on Carolyn's sofa, recalling the dream; recalling the fear actually, rather than the dream itself. The strange midnight terror that permeates the bones while your mind, alert and rational, insists that all is as normal, there is nothing to be frightened of. But that bone-fear that belongs to sleep is deaf to reason and continues to quake, in dread, I suppose, of darkness and death. At any rate, it seems after a while to have nothing any longer to do with the substance of the dream that created it.

I don't describe my dreams to Dr Taylor any more. Now I say, 'I had another dream,' and he nods. Then we sit in silence for a while allowing, as it were, the dream to pass. I'm grateful to him for that, relieved that he has stopped searching for meaning and allows me simply to describe the order of my life. How it works. I agreed to see him once a week as an outpatient in return for coming off the pills they insisted I took even after I left the hospital. I am glad that he seems to have understood now that I'm functioning well and no longer tries to get 'to the bottom of things'. As I see it breakdowns of the mind are not so very different from those of the body. Subjected to stress, unfamiliar situations and so on, both are likely to be disturbed. Also I think there may be a genetic factor, a biochemical fault that predisposes certain people to particular kinds of malfunction. It's perfectly understandable without the need to delve into the past. I think the archeologists of the mind are no more successful at interpreting the leftovers of the past than the sort who dig the earth. Both come up with interesting and plausible stories, but they are no more than speculation. I prefer the present, the sense of a job to be done, life to be got on with. It's much more important to be effective than to wonder endlessly, why, why, why? Certainly I was ill, but time and medication made me better. I feel well and able to cope. To want to analyse the past is to suggest a continuous malfunction. It is only their ignorance of the structure of the brain which sends them in this direction. Their pitiful inability to understand what actually has gone wrong. Even Freud, I believe, said that his theory was no more than a holding operation until the chemistry of the brain had been better analysed. We're still waiting, it seems.

I don't mind seeing Dr Taylor, especially now that he has accepted my position. It's a regular part of my life, and I enjoy describing the pattern of my days to him.

When I left Carolyn's flat in the late afternoon I was feeling much better and decided to walk home. A brisk walk in the cold, dry air, past the urban camels and zebras, their breath clouding around their nostrils, and along the canal with its moored restaurants and art galleries, back into the cityscape of Swiss Cottage and through the dark Victorian back-streets to the confusion of Kentish Town and the simplicity of my flat.

Twelve

Mo felt strong and clear in the forest and moved through it in her practical jungle boots, strong olive-green trousers and shirt, with confidence and efficiency. The slump of the previous weeks evaporated into the saturated, tropical air. Her feeling of depression, of heaviness, which her GP assured her was the usual aftereffect of mononucleosis, lifted as soon as her plane had taken off. And the peculiar reaction she had had to her mother's revelation – the breathlessness, the feeling of something blocking the upper part of her chest – was gone. She had not thought about her family since she had walked into the airport. Mo felt herself again, her own person, doing her job, living her life. Taking the next step in her career. There was nobody, she thought as she settled into her seat on the plane, that she missed at all. It was a thought that pleased her.

After two days at the research station she left with Leloh to go upriver to Sub-Camp 3. Her plan was to spend two weeks there alone, working on her grids, then to return to Base Camp for a few days for a break. And so on. Her periods at Base Camp would allow her to renew supplies, pick up and send mail, and use the radio to order whatever she needed. It was not good, she knew, to spend too much time alone in the forest interior. One might get out of touch, begin to lose sight in some way of the threads she hoped would come together into a final pattern. And she would need the easy camaraderie of the others at the station, just as she needed to drop into the staff common room at college from time to time to chat to the others in the department, seemingly about nothing very much.

Leloh dropped her off at the sub-camp and helped her unload the things from the boat. Then he left, smiling and promising to return in a fortnight to take her back to Base Camp.

She worked hard in the late afternoon light, emptying crates and carrying her supplies into the tent, setting up her desk and mosquito netting over the camp bed, stacking everything neatly as she went along. As she was about to unpack the final crate the tiny clearing fell, in an instant, into deep shadow, as black weighted clouds seemed to arrive from nowhere and blot out the sky. Thunder rumbled and then cracked above her head as the clouds burst and torrential rain deluged the whole area, including Mo's tent, designed to withstand the daily downpour, but lashed and buffeted by the sudden wind and drummed on as though a full orchestra of snare drums were greeting her arrival. Mo, already drenched, ran to the tent, one of the creatures that found what shelter it could until the storm had passed. Monkeys clung miserably to a sturdy branch in the canopy, their sodden fur plastered to their bodies; ants and termites, those that were not drowned in the sudden flowing riverlets, scuttled back to their holes and nests; spiders hung on tightly to their webs and some were not washed away. Animal life was stilled. Creatures that had no place to retreat to, or burrows to dig into, stood with statue-like acceptance waiting for an end to the tempest. The other, inanimate life of the forest danced frantically to the whistling wind and the weight of water that fell like a solid mass from the sky, heavily on to the canopy, then down in stages through the gaps on to millions of leaves, shaped so that the water streamed from their pointed tips, down further into layer after layer of the forest. Whole trees crashed to the ground, their shallow roots unable to withstand the pressure of the sheeting wind and rain; branches broke off and fell a hundred feet to the forest floor taking with them other, smaller branches, ripping down leaves and lianas as they went – all to provide new food for the millipedes and other soil animals that assisted the process of decay and regrowth once the rain had ceased. Mo was part of the stillness of animal life in her tent, waiting and smelling the drenched greenness and the flooded soil that made the already hot, wet air almost unbreathable.

When the thunder had died into the distance and the clouds rolled away as suddenly as they had arrived, there was silence for a few moments. An extraordinary absence of sound fell over the forest, broken only by the noise of residual water dripping from level to level. Mo sat on her camp bed, hushed herself, not unmoved by the drama that had played out around her, this daily catastrophe, life-giving and destructive all at once.

Mo's return from the northern seasonal place was noted by the rainforest whose elements again included her in its existence. The rain had fallen on her too, and had been minutely affected by her presence. What had fallen on her had fallen nowhere else, its down-ward path altered and deflected by her being there, just as its route was defined by the other obstacles of tree, leaf and creature it encountered. Her breathing changed the levels in the atmosphere; her footsteps affected the scurrying insect life and the structure of the forest floor. Again her body shifted and blocked light, made shadow, and creatures scampered and scuttled away as their ears and scent organs registered her existence.

But still, as far as Mo was concerned, she was *in* the forest, *she* experienced *it*, and had no notion of the forest in her, experiencing her. The rainforest welcomed that part of itself that was Mo, but Mo sensed nothing of the communication. It was not nearness or dis-tance that made her deaf to it. Now that she was in it she was actually no closer to it than she had been in the concrete streets of Bloomsbury and Kentish Town.

It took Mo most of the first fortnight to set out her pattern of grids on the forest floor, marking out the squares with tough nylon string and pegs cut from fallen branches, then transferring the pattern on to graph paper and describing the topography within each square in her field work notebook. She paced out and pegged two 15 metre-square plots, separated by an hour's trek, which she then sub-divided, marking out ten 1.5 metre quadrats in each. Then she began the detailed noting and identification of everything growing in each sub-section. Measuring the diameter and estimating the height of the trees and lianas, listing all the flora in every quadrat and taking representative samples for drying of ferns, mosses, groundherbs and leaves – everything that grew to a height of three metres above ground. She spent the evenings in the tent transferring lists to the paper grids and tabulating her collections. The purpose of her study was twofold. Firstly, to make a survey of a representative section of primary rainforest by collecting and quantifying whatever she found growing within her set of squares; and secondly to make some assessment of the rate of decomposition of the litter on the forest floor in order to understand better the nutritional chain that maintained the forest's existence. The latter study she set in motion halfway through her first fortnight at the sub-camp by placing mesh sacks of varying gauges within a random selection of quadrats. Whatever they contained would be collected at regular intervals, sorted, dried and weighed. The comparative results from the litterbags would tell her not only the rate of decomposition of various materials, but also the relative importance of soil animals as against chemical action in the process of decay, since the varying meshes were designed, some to filter out, some to trap the termites, millipedes and woodlice that played a central part in the recycling of nutrients. How central their role was, was something she intended her project to reveal.

So Mo worked.

The hiss of the pressure lamp she worked by mingled with the clamour of the forest: the howls and wails of birds and mammals, the continual pulsating clicks of the cicadas, the raucous lament of the frogs. The night-time noise of the forest was so intense, so densely packed, that it finally came to represent silence to Mo, and took on the same familiar night-blanketing quality of the Sussex countryside silence she had grown up with. Long-ago evenings of quiet application, reading, doing homework, listening to the clock ticking the darkness away, were not so very different from being bent over her worktable in the tent, analysing and calculating; the wild sounds outside no more disturbing to her than the wind gusting around the old brick house and the occasional cry of an owl in the fields beyond her garden. Sometimes, in the night, she woke startled by an unearthly shriek and lay for a second paralysed with fear, suddenly cold and clammy in spite of the saturating heat, but in a moment she would recognize the enclosing mosquito net and remember where she was, and the terror would subside with the knowledge that such cries were normal here, part of the environment and not to be feared. She would slip back into sleep by running over a list of possible identities for the creature whose call she had heard – a jungle version of counting sheep.

It was necessary to be exceptionally orderly in the forest. At the end of a day's collecting, sweat-soaked clothes had to be hung high from the tent roof to keep them from invading insects, and the dry evening set unpacked from their protective plastic. When she made a meal, all loose food immediately had to be resealed and replaced in moisture- and ant-proof containers once she had measured out her portion. The forest and its inhabitants threatened to be everywhere, inside, under, on everything; the damp rotting, the insects crawling, so that nothing could be left casually about, out or open. Mo was never caught out as others had been, finding fire ants drunk with well-being in the precious store of muesli, or relenting, just once, and climbing luxuriously, against all good advice, into the only clean, dry and warm set of clothing one morning instead of the ever-wet working set, only to suffer for the rest of the study period with two sets of sodden, smelly, undryable clothes. She made no mistakes of that kind, and maintained as methodical an attitude to her day to day existence as she did to her information grids. When she had finished her day's work and put away her papers and graphs, she climbed underneath the mosquito net on to her camp bed with a book, or a pad to write letters home; reassuring ones to her mother, interesting accounts of her surroundings and the current findings of her project to Luke. She felt very remote from England and the people there. Writing the letters was like being a contented castaway putting messages in a bottle and chucking them out to sea. She had no sense of them actually being read, no sense of the real existence of others in another place continuing a life that was once familiar enough to her. Had she been a castaway she would not have put a return address on her messages.

The rainforest watched Mo's activities and found them unaccountable. Living in her tent with her damp-proof, insect-proof, forest-proof containers she seemed at war with the very essence of the place. The shapes she mapped out on the ground, squares within squares, were not the shapes of nature, marked out, as they were, with an unknown liana that neither lived nor died, nor gave anything of itself. The watching was strange enough, but the pattern of watching more alien still: the daily visits with notebook and pencil, certain squares visited and noted one day, others the next. There was a pattern to her behaviour, but one that bore no relation to the patterns of the forest and its inhabitants. The trees flowered according to the ambient conditions, each species having its own requirements so that when flowering could happen, it did. At any time of the year there were simultaneously flowers, fruit, buds, leaf fall, depending on need and possibility. A leech would lurk hidden on a branch or beneath the giant blade of a fern for hours or days, waiting for a chemical signal that life, warm blood was close by. Then it would stiffen and reach out, extended to what seemed an impossible length to clamp its mouth part on to whatever creature happened by. But like the trees, the leech waited for its moment to gorge itself and swell to several times its size when its chance came. There was no regular pattern, only the irregular pattern of necessity. If a tree fell and provided light and space, seeds that had lain buried in the forest floor, quiescent for months, would sprout and throw up shoots within hours. Everything was ready, everything waited. And often leeches died, since nothing passed by soon enough, and seeds rotted, their potential returning to the soil to benefit the existing trees because no gap had occurred. For all that, the forest went on;

chance provided enough opportunity for the continuation of life. But Mo plodded around her grids in her set routines, measuring how much litter fell in two-week intervals, or how much growth had occurred on the 1.5 metre plots that were checked every Tuesday. All of it meaningless to the forest that knew everything about cycles of life and death, but nothing about time and measurement.

Mo was not, of course, the first member of her species to have entered the awareness of the forest. For millenia hunters and gatherers had inhabited the place, and at least at first, they had lived much as the other creatures lived; as part of the pattern, taking food from the trees, hunting mammals as other predators did, using the substance of the forest to survive and returning their own substance when life ended. But quite soon they were burning and hacking small areas away to clear the ground and grow crops. The system adjusted itself quite easily since the impoverished soil, its nutrients leeched by forest growth and flood, would not sustain crops for long once the cycle of decay and rapid growth had been broken. So the slashers and burners moved on every few seasons to another part of the forest and within a few years the bare patch was covered with leafy tangled growth and indistinguishable from its surroundings.

Then, much more recently, the developers had come with great machines that belched fumes and tore vast tracts of forest down in hours: trees fell like matchsticks for the loggers and became timber, and the naked, dead land was transformed into concrete roads and cities. And yet the burners and the wreckers with their machines were still within the grasp of the forest. They used it without consideration, just as the forest did not consider itself. Neither the local farmers nor the developers pondered the nature of the place, or their place within nature; they simply accepted it for what it was, part of where they were, like the rest of the life that made up the totality of the forest. They used it, like everything else did. While the numbers were small, the burning and crop growing caused no imbalance in the system. But even now, when millions of acres were destroyed, when the entire existence of the forest was threatened, a natural relationship remained. The forest was not partial when it came to life and death. Having no time, no sense of first beginnings and final endings, it did not mourn its approaching non-existence. It could not mourn. A cell, or an eagle's death, just *was*. Its own end was of no greater significance. If the creatures that had begun as hunters like any other had become predators so numerous and powerful that they would wipe out the rainforest, then so be it. They had become that way, after all, through their capacity to take and use the environment for their own advantage. They were what they were. It was the measure of success of a species, and this one only did particularly well what the rest attempted. It was not the nature of the forest to ponder the global consequences of its own destruction, especially when those consequences meant no more than the ending of the sovereignty of one species and the beginning of yet another cycle of life on the planet. Another ending, another beginning. A small moment in eternity. So it would be.

But the scientists were different. They visited the forest without becoming part of it. They measured and looked, and if they took away only information they took more than the most destructive of the other humans. For they remained outside and therefore inexplicible. They noted and preserved and conserved, and in doing so denied any connection between their own singular existence and the substance of the forest. They were not part of the natural world, but its guardian. They were alien as no other aspect of life could be. Destruction – a creature's need to use the environment even to its detriment – was within the process of life as the forest understood it. This other way, the watching, unconnected way, could not be comprehended.

Thirteen

It was all making more and more sense, becoming a coherent pattern.

Mo tended her squares of forest on the two sites, each square numbered and visited in a regular order. She measured the growth of everything within the designated quadrats and compared rates between the separated sites. She collected the litterbags from the decomposition study squares every fortnight and weighed and dried the material back at Base Camp. The weight loss within and between each site was measured and compared, and she began to see a picture emerging of the extraordinary speed of decay on the forest floor, and the vital role of the living creatures that inhabited that level of the environment. Mo was not excessively interested in analysing figures at this point, that was for later, back at the university. The time in the forest was for collecting data and this she did scrupulously.

Every morning, after she had cleared her breakfast away, she pulled on her rucksack and trudged out to Site One, the nearer of the two. Now, after three months, she had worn the beginnings of a path between the clearing and the grids. A line from here to there where her persistent footfalls prevented normal growth and decay. It was a winding path as she had skirted round the strongly grown saplings and thick clumps of fern, or a decaying tree trunk that was now home for millions of termites and woodlice. There were miniature versions of Mo's path everywhere in the forest made by columns of determined soldier ants that marched to and from food sources, or to make war on the less organized insects.

Mo's body had acclimatized somewhat to the heat and humidity, but still, on the hour-long trek to the first site, and the second hour to the next, she sweated heavily and breathed with difficulty. The humidity count after a storm could be ninety-eight per cent she knew, and sometimes she felt as if she were indeed just two per cent away from drowning. The smell, too, always hit her anew as she entered the forest from her clearing. The subtle stench of rot. Damp, decaying leaves, their flesh mildewed. Pieces of bark softened by the wet air and soil and broken down by tiny animals that gained sustenance from them. And the powerful odour from bizarrely shaped fungi, phalluses and intricate latticework that pushed up through the composting mulch. The smell of the forest, at once sharp and deep, a mingling of all the stages of life from fresh young growth to putrefaction. The very air seemed sometimes to be mouldering, its molecules imprisoned by the heat and moisture. It would have been, in any other circumstances, a terrible smell, one which, had it come from her mother's kitchen, would have had her scrubbing and disinfecting and calling in Rentokil to spray away chemically the dreadful and vibrant stench of life and death.

It was true that the sombre misted grey-green light, the soaked air, the smell, even the shiny, thick texture of the forest leaves were oppressive, and Mo, who was not one for allowing her environment to dictate her mood, had occasionally to fight down a sense of awful isolation and loneliness on those early morning walks. But she knew a more objective attitude was necessary and right. The stench was the very stuff of her project, the essence, in every sense, of the place. Mo had never expected to feel comfortable in the forest, and being hardy, as well as sensible, was usually able to dissociate herself from the humanly unpleasant aspects of her surroundings. There was nothing personal about the discomfort. It was the nature of the place. But still, it was not surprising that most of humanity chose not to live in such an environment.

During her periods back at Base Camp Mo took the opportunity to soak her dirty work clothes and to wash her hair, cut a little shorter and usually, when on site, tied back and pushed under a floppy-brimmed canvas hat. She soaped herself in the cleverly constructed shower behind the long house and then, on her first evening back, sat fresh and clean, her hair hanging loose and fly-away from the static of her energetic brush strokes. She would sit in her small compartment-room of the long house, looking through her notebook to see what supplies she would have to order over the radio and reading any mail that had arrived since her last visit.

The others at the station always welcomed her back with a feast of freshly caught fish from the river, pleased to turn the evening's quiet talk into something a little more convivial. They sat around the wooden table in what they called the dining area, and asked Mo about conditions down at Sub-Camp 3, how she was managing, if the project was going according to plan. Then they would give her their news – of first-ever sightings, new species discovered and now named after their proud finder, his name forever guaranteed a place in some obscure corner of biological science. Or a medical drama; a local boy, bitten by a krait and airlifted to the nearest hospital by the helicopter they had radioed for; or a woman from Leloh's village saved from certain death by the antibiotics they had taken to her. Later, drinking beer or the local fermented brew, they would tell each other stories of their past and sing songs. Mo, temporarily, was the only woman among the six who were using the station. The men, on the whole, dealt with her singular female presence by conferring honorary masculinity on her within the group, and she did nothing public – like wearing 'feminine' clothes, or being especially helpful when it came to the preparation of food, or generally using her body in anything other than a practical way – to disturb this attitude. It was politic and in any case to her taste.

But there was one man there, an Australian ornithologist called Derek, whom she seemed to talk to more than the others. They had struck up a pleasant friendship over the weeks when their visits back to Base Camp happened to coincide. He was a large, quiet, smiling man in his thirties, boyish and passionate in his devotion to his particular field of research, which was to seek out and record all the possible species of a nocturnal bird call a frogmouth.

The others at the camp came to recognize that Mo and Derek had a friendship going, but since there were no strong undercurrents that disturbed the group, the pairing served, if anything, to maintain the harmony within the small community. Mo, being 'taken', could not now be considered available for any passing erotic thoughts that might arise.

One night Derek invited Mo to join him on one of his midnight expeditions in search of a so far unrecorded species of frogmouth he was certain inhabited the forest, but had yet to have an actual sighting of.

Mo followed him into the pitch-black forest, surprised at his dexterity as he tracked through the undergrowth, his large, booted feet hardly cracking a twig, and the body that seemed positively to lumber back at Base Camp sliding stealthily between giant ferns and ducking overhanging lianas. She followed his dark form, trying for an equal silence without success. Sometimes Derek stopped suddenly and shone a flashlight up into the canopy where he had heard a rustle of leaves, a fluttering of tiny wings in the still, hot air. The beam made a vertical path through the trees and foliage, but was always empty; there was never more than the merest flash of some-thing that had been, but was not there any longer, as the night creatures of the forest fled back into the darkness.

They walked for an hour or more and every now and then Derek put his finger to his mouth and emitted a tiny whistle, like a plaintive kitten complaining of neglect. Sometimes, in the far distance, there was an echo, and Derek would turn and head in the direction of the sound. Finally his call was returned and repeated, a little closer, then closer still, as Derek became a tree, immobile, lifeless, until the mewing could be heard almost above their heads. He made a low wave to signal complete silence to Mo and then turned his flashlight into the tree, and there was the silhouette of something minute, flying from branch to branch, obscured by leaves and shadow and impossible to identify with any certainty, but there, definitely there. Derek was delighted, and whooped with joy. It was enough for the night, frogmouths were rarely sighted and the evening had assured him that they were there to be found.

When they got back to camp it was three in the morning. Derek brewed up a celebratory cup of cocoa for them both and sloshed in a generous helping of brandy. They carried their cups into Derek's section of the long house, so as not to disturb the others, and sat on his bed sipping their drink, Derek still glowing with the satisfaction of the search and the faint shadow that had promised more.

'Wasn't it marvellous? Wasn't it bloody marvellous?' he grinned at Mo. And she grinned back with equal excitement. She too had felt the special privilege of being in that special place deep in the night, and the excitement of finding what one was looking for.

'It was wonderful. Thank you for taking me. I'm sorry I was so clumsy out there. I felt like an ox lumbering about.'

'Oh, don't worry about it. It takes time to get used to the forest at night. There's a trick. You have to put your eyes in your feet.' Mo laughed. 'No, really. You have to let your feet do the seeing. They can, if you trust them. I am glad you liked it.'

Then there was a shift in the atmosphere. Derek's eyes changed as he looked at her, became damp with pleasure rather than gleaming with excitement, and the air seemed to hum with a new tension. Gentle and shy as he was, he looked at her now with a directness that was unavoidable, like the beam from his torch, and then he reached out a hand to stroke the side of her hair.

Mo pulled sharply to one side.

'Don't,' she said. She could feel the excitement of the forest search turning to sexuality in her; she wanted him naked against her, to feel him close and the tensed muscles of his back under her hand. She wanted the expertise and delicacy he had shown tracking through the dark forest to work on her. 'Don't,' she said, as he pulled her gently towards him. She wrenched away. 'Don't,' she repeated.

'Why, Mo? What's the matter?' he asked, his hand still touching her hair.

'Because . . . I don't want to,' she explained. 'It's not a good idea . . . to . . . get involved.'

'Why? We're both adults. We want each other.'

'It's not *necessary*,' she said firmly. 'We've both got work to do. I don't think it's a good idea.'

Derek looked at her for a moment. 'All right,' he said eventually. 'If that's what you want.'

Mo smiled and pulled back her hair over her forehead. 'Thanks for this evening. It was really marvellous. Good night.'

She took the two mugs of cocoa back into the main room and stacked them by the washing-up bowl, then went to her section of the long house and to bed.

She was pleased she had allowed the moment to pass. It would have been easy to take Derek's gentle affection, but that was not what she was there for. If part of her wanted to be held and touched, most of her did not. The idea of being inside a pair of male arms made her almost dizzy with rage. The anger carried her through the desire and now it had, she was glad of it.

The next morning there was a mail drop. Mo had two letters, the first she had received since her arrival. One was from her mother, she knew the handwriting. She put it to one side and opened the other. She thought it might be from Luke. In fact it came from Liam.

'My dear Mo,' it began, and she could almost see his eyes squeezing closed as his pen hovered over the light airmail paper. 'How I miss your severe presence. I picture you strong and sturdy, striding through your forest, cutting it down to size. You aren't, I hope, taming *all* the mystery out of it – I'd like to think there's a small pocket of resistance in the world that simply won't be understood. Couldn't you allow just one insignificant species to remain unknown? An ant with no name, perhaps? A fern that has no obvious function within your gloriously tidy system? Just for me? For old friendship's sake?

'I see you looking impatient at my frivolity. You're right, I suppose – everything must be known and put in its proper place – how else are we to understand the world? You see, I can do it too. I do believe I need you nearby to disagree with. Without you to argue against my own position starts to seem very weak. Whatever you may say about the underlying order of nature, we humans are in a bloody mess. We could agree on that – with the exception, of course, of you, my dear, sensible friend.

'We are still friends, aren't we? In spite of my folly?

'My news then. You'll want to hear of my sorrow and regret, but, shamefully, I'm basking in Grace's sunlight. Of course, I'm a bloody liar. I'm also sick with guilt and loss – my lovely flowing family are stiff and polite, as if they've all lost heart. I've torn the heart out of them. Not the baby, of course, but I fancy she imbibes Sophie's sadness and anger along with her milk.

'I do understand the damage I've done. It's as if I've been in a fatal accident – too messy to assess blame, but someone's been killed and I'll have to live with the memory, the sight of pain and death. Serve me right, you'll say – I know you have no trouble in apportioning blame. But although there's no question that it's my fault, I can't say I'm actually to blame. No, no one else either. How I long for the simple sixties when a throw of the yarrow sticks would have assured me of no blame. I'm stuck in the past, not that it's an especially valuable past, only that the present *says* nothing at all. The sixties said "no blame", and even if it was wrong, at least it wasn't silence.

'My God, Mo, it's not easy maintaining a commitment to self-loathing – do you think perhaps that is the single quality that distinguishes us from the animals? Not the acquisition of language, or tool-use, or walking on our hind legs, but a capacity for self-loathing? Is there any other creature in creation that can do that – look at itself and feel disgust? Perhaps we could collaborate on a paper addressing the subject.

'Grace does not have a natural talent for domestic bliss. Passionate encounters in her tutor's office were what she wanted. I, as ever,

want everything. Passion and domesticity. Serenity and sex. Being
very old, I see the attraction of both sides. Grace, being much older,
knows instinctively that it's one thing or the other.

'So we fight, which I, naturally, adore. I weep and beg forgiveness
while she glares at me with the contempt I know you'll agree I
deserve. Forgiveness for what? For wanting her, and wanting
nothing more than to want her. I *must* have her body: it has become
the single goal in my life. Sometimes she accuses me of using her as a
"sex object", having read some appropriate tracts in Layla's
wretched course on Feminism and Anthropology at college. She
says, "You don't love me at all, it's only my body you're interested
in." Dear God, we are living in a circle of hell, and she is worrying
about my sexist attitude. It's like an inhabitant of Hades complaining that it doesn't rain often enough.

'My obsession has dragged us both to the lowest places of human
interaction. To call it animal would libel the natural world. Our life
together is at once a denial of what is human *and* animal in us. I have
distorted nature, found the worst of both worlds in myself and
imprisoned her there. I'm not degrading women, Mo, I'm degrading
humanity. There is only the single, narrow focus on to Grace's body.
I cannot see anything else. Nothing else has meaning any more.

'Eventually, when the shouting is over and I have shed enough
tears, Grace relents and I take her. For me now, sexuality is desper-
ation, merely the dreadful need to have the object of my desire. (I
imagine you have already stopped reading. I won't, however, stop
writing. I will say it all.) She is supremely object. When she permits
my lust and stands, at last, naked in front of me, what I see are
fragments. Her beautiful breasts; the sharp line that runs from hip to
mid-thigh; the crease that divides the inside of her forearm from her
upper arm. There is a precise two inches where the neck runs into
the shoulder that is so indescribably lovely I want to weep, even
now, just thinking about it. Sometimes, if she is willing, I will stand
and gaze at that part of her for minutes on end, for as long as she will
allow me, occasionally running the tip of my forefinger along it, like

a half-blind man trying to perceive the shape of the curve with his sense of touch because his eyes cannot take it in sufficiently.

'All the desirable parts of her are separate; I want each, not all. And the parts never become a whole. If she has a cold, which she often does, and her nose is red and raw, her eyes puffy, positively rheumy, it has no effect on my desire. Truly, I wouldn't care if she were leprous, so long as the pieces of her that I want remain intact. What will I do when her tits begin to sag, and the cellulite makes the perfect line of her hip and thigh indistinct? I want her forever, but as she is now. It is her particular, precise configuration of cells that I want. Of course, there are other bodies whose parts are as beautiful, but I can't want them. My lovely Sophie, or a thousand passing bodies whose owners I do not know. If I could flit from girl to girl like a humming bird, sipping at this flower, then that, at least the damage would be lessened to each. Or if I could want Sophie, whose whole person I know and love. I can't, I can't. I'm blind to everything but the bits of my Grace. They fit into my empty spaces like a chemical key. As one takes a specific antibiotic that imitates the shape of a virus in order to suppress its action, I take the pieces of Grace to prevent the spreading infection of emptiness.

'And the child complains of my sexism. Has there ever been a grosser underestimation of a crime?

'I want you to know this about me, Mo, my dear, because I think you will understand, if you can allow yourself. You with your grids and labels and measurements. Do you think we are so very different, differently gendered though we are? We each use our fetishism in different areas, but perhaps, in the end, we are trying to avoid the same thing.

'We are going to get married. She says I must marry her to prove I really love her. A commitment, she says. If she only knew how dreadful a commitment I already have. But I am getting a divorce and we *will* be married, because I want to make it up to her. It's something I can do that she wants. We will, of course, be unhappy, and I will have to watch her growing older, and, I suppose, someone will come along eventually who will love her properly, and she will understand what is missing between us and leave me. It's my dread and comfort. There must be punishment, mustn't there, Mo?

'In the meantime I do everything necessary to ensure that she is available to me. I do most of the shopping and cooking, and pay the bills. I take her, to the embarrassment of my friends, to dinner parties, and, to the embarrassment of myself, to the theatre and exhibitions, not because she enhances the event, but because this, for her, is the way couples behave. You understand she is not exceptionally stupid. If that were so she might provide an original view of life. She is merely ordinary and utterly conventional in her thinking. So I make sure, for her sake, and therefore mine, that all the trappings of coupledom are there and ask only for access to her body in return.

'Forgive this late-night ramble, Mo, and God forgive me my inability to do anything else. Clearly I would have made a poor mystic. I lack all control. I've caged myself inside one of your squares. Perhaps, after all, it's the only safe place to be.

'Take care of yourself, my dear. My regards to the rainforest.

'Your friend, Liam.'

Mo sat on her bed, her newly clean hair wrapped in a towel, staring at the sheet of airmail paper in her hand. She read the letter a second time, while the set line of her mouth indicated her response. There was instantaneous anger and disgust as her eyes, then her brain took in the words on the page; but there was also something else. Not pity, he had enough of his own already and, in any case, deserved none. Of course he was to blame, how could he deny it? Who else? Not Grace clearly, who seemed not to know what she had got herself into, and certainly not Sophie. Of course he was to blame. He presented himself as an existential hero, spiralling down to the abyss. Self-aggrandizing rubbish! To turn such damaging indulgence into a mystical quest was disgusting. There was no justification for hurting people like that. Better to keep away from people altogether if pain was all you gave them in the end. Pain and deception.

But beneath the righteous anger lay another feeling, barely conscious: understanding. There was something in the description of his sexuality that she recognized. Not as sexuality but, just for a second, reading his attempt to link them, he with his compulsive fetishism, she with her scientific partitioning of nature, she understood the connection he was making, and perhaps better than he did himself. Only for a flash though. As soon as the feeling, and it was no more than that, asserted itself, anger welled again. How dare he equate her professional techniques with his pathetic lust? It was nonsense. Liam was no more than a self-conscious version of Joe, grabbing what he wanted, caring nothing, not really, for the consequences. If either of them cared, they wouldn't do it. It was as simple as that.

Well, she cared. If she cut up the forest, it was so that she could put it back together again with greater understanding. So that she could conserve, look after a vulnerable ecological system. There was no connection. None.

It was the forest in Mo that received, via her brain decoding the words, Liam's meaning and understood its import. So the human organism did this to everything then, including members of its own species. This information was vital, making sense of the incomprehensible facts the forest had stored away as 'disturbance of the organism' during its observation of Mo. At last there was coherence. This, then, was what people were. It cleared up the mystery, gave the underlying source of the strangeness it had seen and failed to understand. The forest did not ask itself 'why' this single species should be as it is. 'Why' was not included in the forest's meditations. It needed only to know what was. Now Mo was no longer an aberration in nature, but an example of the condition of her form of life. The notion of fetishism came to represent the very nature of the human species. The sexual, scientific, and social behaviour of the life form could be encompassed within such a concept. These extraordinary creatures that used *things* to understand the planet, made a *thing* of the planet and of each other in the process. It was of no concern, no relevance, to the forest that they subdivided thing-making into good and bad. The forest noted from Mo's reactions that this was the case; that she experienced Liam's sexual fetishism as a 'bad' thing, whereas her activities in the world, being based on a desire to study and conserve, were a 'good' thing. The forest, unconcerned with human rationality, knew that it was the *thing-making* that was the source from which all else stemmed. They were remarkable, unique beings; animals that were outside everything, including themselves. Had the forest been able to feel fear, it would have trembled at so alien a concept, but lacking emotion was simply enriched by its increased knowledge. And not being human, it did not seek to use its new information. What was, was.

Mo put Liam's letter to one side and lay back on the camp bed before she began slowly to open the envelope that bore her mother's handwriting. With this one, at least, she was prepared for annoyance. Her eyes skimmed quickly over the first paragraphs of anxious enquiry – was she ill, terribly lonely, couldn't she write more often? The first part of the letter was a blur of worry. It was the setting down of anxiety. That was the point, Mo thought, since, after all, by the time the letter reached her, it was no longer relevant if three weeks ago she had been ill, or had a moment of anguish, and anyway her last letter had crossed Marjorie's in the post. The inevitable time lapse made a nonsense of such urgent concerns. The real situation was not the point. When one looked out to a star that no longer existed, was the reality the fact that one saw an object in the sky, or the equally real fact that it was not actually there? The reality here was Marjorie's need to express the sentiment. What if she wrote back to say she had dysentery – which, by the time Marjorie read of it back in the south of England, would no longer be true? The questions were not real questions and the answers would not be real answers. But, she thought guiltily, her mother was only expressing her concern for her daughter in conventional terms; it did no harm. She wished there were someone, though, who would take a scientific interest in what she was doing, and ask her for details of her research. Her father would have been interested in what she was doing.

She stopped reading and began now to imagine an exchange of letters between them. He would write back with theories based on her findings, talk to people at the university who were in the field and write to her of the discussions they had in the common room. Perhaps some passing comment would shed new light and offer an entirely different way of approaching the material. Of course, Sheila would take an interest and send her best wishes. Might he not actually come out on a visit for a couple of weeks? Having his daughter in a rainforest in Borneo would be an unmissable opportunity for a man with such intellectual curiosity. She imagined him arriving in Leloh's longboat to her tent in the clearing and showing him her pattern of squares, then the graphs. Sitting in the lamplit tent, sipping tea, heads close together in mutual fascination with the meaning of the charts and tables. The two of them, equal now, both adults, sharing the pleasure of discovering more about the world. He would look up from the papers on the makeshift desk and smile at her, his eyes gleaming with pride and pleasure as they had when he told her of meals and conversations he'd had with Sheila. 'My clever darling,' he whispered, and stroked her hair gently, easing her head closer, to rest on his shoulder.

For this second, Mo was precariously between daydream and sleep, and they were no longer in the tent in the clearing, but close together in the dim green shadow of the forest interior, standing within a square of the chessboard of nylon string she had laid out on the forest floor. She began to feel the pressure of his body against her and an urgent tension low in her pelvis. Instantly, her eyes blinked open, and she struggled her way back through the weight of sleep, through the leafy layers of forest, up and up towards the source of light that filtered through the canopy, in spite of its density. She pushed herself up into consciousness, back into reality, and the dream, the feeling, the urgency, disappeared.

She had fallen asleep for a moment. She was reading her mother's letter. She had simply lost her place for a second.

Mo shook away the remnants of sleep, the dream now vanished, disappeared from existence, and sat up. The letter was crushed in her closed fist. She smoothed out the creases as well as she could and read on.

'I'm sorry, darling,' the letter continued. 'I'm being silly and fussy, I know. I'm sure you're doing wonderfully. I can almost hear you telling me how irrational I am about your jungle. You're right, I'm sure. All the pictures I see in my head when I think of you there are from old films and newsreels. You know – Japanese prisoner of war camps and more recent things in Vietnam. Now I think about it, I suppose it was what was happening in the jungle, not the place itself that was dreadful. From your letter it's obvious that you and your friends at the research station are very organized and objective and it's not the same at all.

'It's only that I miss you and you seem very far away.

'Your description of gridding and your visits to your plots in rotation made it sound a bit like gardening really. As if you've got an allotment you visit and tend. Of course, I know you aren't growing anything, or doing anything to the environment, but perhaps collecting your information is not too much unlike harvesting fruit and vegetables. I think of you often when I'm in our garden, pruning and weeding and trimming the edges of the lawn. I've been thinking that I might make a wild patch at the back, where our garden meets the meadow. Up to the fence. What do you think? I could sow some wild flower seeds at random, just scatter them about, and allow the weeds to grow – and just see what happens. Perhaps it would coax some of the wildlife from the meadow across the fence to visit. Of course I love Daddy's lawn and damask roses; I love to look after them and keep them just so, but perhaps there's also room for another kind of garden, something with less definite edges. I imagine the scents and colours mingling and drawing birds and butterflies. Very chaotic, but lovely. An accidental garden. A glorious surprise. What do you think?

'I was listening the other day to the radio when a programme came on about widows. How there are so many women left alone because men seem to die first, and how difficult it is to adjust to being alone, often for the first time in a woman's life. I don't think I'd quite thought of it like that before. It suddenly seemed as if I was having an exciting new adventure. One poor woman on the programme said that in the twenty years since her husband had died, she had felt she was just waiting out her life. Marking time, because his death meant that everything was over. Just imagine, Mo, twenty years! That's a quarter of a lifetime. And then I thought that it was fifteen years since Daddy had died, and she was quite right, I'd been doing the same thing, really. But there's a different way of looking at it. That this was something new to learn and enjoy – and in fact I've been enjoying it without actually knowing I was. Living alone, making my own choices, not having to fit in, or consult with anyone else when I want to go for a walk, or about what to eat, and when to sleep. Do you know sometimes I stay up all night? Simply because I want to and there's no need to get up at a particular time. And really, that's such a pleasure when you've never done it before. Naturally, I loved being with Daddy and with you, but this is different, and in its own way, very satisfactory. It's very completing somehow. Do you understand? You must, since you've known what it is to be independent. I'm so glad you've been able to have time on your own while you're young. It takes much longer to learn things when you're older if you've had no practice. I think Daddy would be rather proud of me, don't you? I'm rather proud of me! I sometimes think that the most perfect thing would have been to have found this out when Daddy was still with me. I don't quite know how we could have lived together *and* had the chance to each live our own private lives, but I feel quite certain that it must be possible to achieve. In a funny sort of way though, I think perhaps he had less privacy than anyone, what with being married, and his closeness to you, and then when he was free of us, his friendship with the woman at the university. He can't have had much time of his own at all, he filled it all up with company. I don't think he knew how to be alone, and I'm sorry he missed out on that. Suddenly I feel that I've been very lucky. Does that sound dreadful? It isn't, really. I only mean to say that I'm enjoying life..

'Perhaps that's what I want to ask you, really – are you enjoying your jungle? I know you're wonderfully independent and capable and good at your job, but I want to think of you enjoying it too. I wish in your next letter you'd give me more details. What it's really like. What are you actually doing in your study? You say such general things, it's very hard to get a picture of you being there on a day to day basis. How *do* you study a rainforest? And what do you do when you're not working?

'Do write back soon, I love to hear from you, darling, and you're in my thoughts a good deal.

'All my love, Mummy.'

There was a PS. 'Incidentally, I've used the key you left me to your flat once or twice, just to stay overnight on the odd trip to London. I haven't disturbed anything and I was sure you wouldn't mind. Love. . .'

Mo unclenched her fist and threw the letter on to the crate that served as a bedside table. Wild gardens . . . staying up all night . . . Daddy unable to be alone . . . enjoying the jungle. Mo simply refused to give this letter any further thought. The expected knot in her diaphragm was present, the annoyance and impatience she had known she would feel reading any letter from Marjorie, but so too, underneath that, and so unexpected that it was not to be defined, was a deep anxiety and distress. Wild gardens . . . staying up all night . . . Daddy unable to be alone . . . enjoying the jungle. Like a route map. Not hers, her mother's. A sketch plan of a journey. But her mother did not make journeys. Nonsense. Another piece of silliness from her idiotic mother. Woodlice in the fire. Nothing to think about. The worry would go away and leave her once again with simple aggravation.

She gave her hair a final vigorous rub with the towel and then brushed it hard and fast, over and over, until the dark strands loaded with static floated around her head, liberated at last from the necessity of falling straight and smooth to her shoulders as if solid fabric and not thousands of individual filaments.

She returned with Leloh the next day to Sub-Camp 3. Derek had been around the previous evening, but there was nothing out of the ordinary about his manner. They chatted pleasantly and the awkwardness of the night before seemed to be forgotten. Mo put it out of her thoughts.

Back in the clearing, in her tent, under the mosquito netting, Mo had, initially, no thoughts at all, except of course for her work. But one night, a few days after her return from Base Camp, she put down her book and settled into the sleeping bag, ready to allow the hum and roar of the forest to lull her into sleep. She lay listening to the pounding rhythms broken by the intermittent shrieks and wails of larger, more individualized creatures, and planned out the following day's work, drifting, as she did so, towards unconsciousness. She felt her muscles relax and the pleasure in her body allowing its full weight to sink into the supporting camp bed, no longer responsible for its bulk. She lay with one arm beneath her head and allowed the other to slip inside the sleeping bag and under the elasticated waistband of her tracksuit, to rest comfortably on her inner thigh. Her brain, like her body, had shut down for the night, and in the dense blackness, relaxed into a restful passivity, received external stimuli – the sounds of the forest, the feel of her hand on her thigh – as if from an immense distance, just ticking over, not analysing or naming anything it picked up.

Her hand stroked the smooth skin like a child playing with a piece of satin, running its thumb along the grain of the material very lightly so that no friction would detract from the slippery feel of the satin on the nerve endings beneath the surface of the skin. Her hand made slow up and down movements over her thigh that brought Mo to the very edge of sleep and she was hardly aware when it moved up slightly to allow her fingers to find her vagina. For a moment they paused, hesitating between her legs, as if surprised at the contrast between the silky skin and the coarse, wiry tangle they now encountered. The forest buzzed outside the tent and Mo's sleep-sodden brain became the sambur deer she had seen on her first journey upriver to this place. It broke through the dense foliage, tangled thickly at the river's edge where the light was not hindered by the sun-darkening canopy. She pushed and nuzzled the draping ropes of lianas out of her path, trampled barricades of sword-shaped ferns and bladelike grasses, stamped saplings, only the thickness of a finger, but branched and laden with heart-shaped leaves, beneath her delicate but determined hooves. She parted the tangled undergrowth of the forest and broke through to the clear daylight of the river, sparkling in the sun, running between the two banks of rampant forest, branches hanging heavily into the water on either side as if trying to conceal the gash. The deer bent and drank from the rushing water, then dashed its muzzle against the surface again and again, each time lifting its head to shake the surplus water from its face, making droplets glisten as they flew through the air to rejoin the river. The sambur drank and frolicked by the river in the phantom daylight of Mo's sleepy brain, as her fingers parted her pubic hair and began to play around her clitoris, moving in time with the rhythm of the forest.

She stroked herself to the beat of the screeching cicadas, then, wet and aroused as her breathing took on the throbbing pace of the frogs, she slipped a finger deep inside herself and moved her hips against the other rhythms of finger and respiration; in counterpoint to the tempo of the forest, but connected, locked into a pattern of sound and movement that was both within her and without, then, finally, neither and both. Her fingers were deft and moved subtly to maintain the growing pressure of pleasure without allowing it to reach its conclusion; lightening her touch as she felt her body ready to release the building tension, waiting for a second to let the intensity drop a notch, because she was not ready and wanted more.

The moment was not yet.

The forest had scored the fugue she played, and she waited, keyed up, the excitement reined in, but ready for the resolution she knew it would provide. A sudden cry tore through the regular beat of the forest as a creature screamed a long, shrill note of death or triumph; a voice from the night forest that ripped through Mo's carefully modulated rhythm, and set off her own abandoned cries to echo back to the dark, wild world outside her tent. The beat inside her swelled and quickened to the climax she had waited for the forest to signal. Her voice pitched high and carrying beyond the walls of her tent into the forest mingled with the other cries. She wanted to call through the forest with a name, or to call the forest by the name, she didn't know which, only that the name belonged out there, re-verberating through the damp, hot night.

Mo slept, having taken the forest into herself, and dreamed green dreams of herself and the forest intertwined, enmeshed, flowing into one another like impossible creatures with no boundaries, a new geometry of fluid form.

But the forest was not taken in. Mo's cries had entered and altered the forest, as did all the activities of anything that existed within its bounds. But for the forest, Mo's cries were no more than a creature making sound. While other things inhabited the place; lived, sought food and mated, gave birth and died, this creature forever remained apart. She took things from the place, did things to it, watched it as if she were no part of it at all. No other living thing stood so outside themselves. Even the use of the sounds of the forest for her own excitement sprang from the structure of her own mind, forcing the separate, unordered sounds into a pattern of her own. A simplification that made many things one – a rhythm, a tempo, not a million individual voices going about their business of staying alive.

The compound eye of the forest noted how Mo had touched herself for the pleasure it had given her, as many creatures touched and played that had enough brain to have the choice. It perceived in her a longing which it understood as the need that was felt when the inner workings of an animal's body required it to find a mate: when the male termite gave up its flight and fell back to the ground on a cloud of guiding scent. The forest knew the imperative, but not the mystery that made it necessary for Mo to be semiconscious before the longing was satisfied. Nor did it understand her making the forest responsible for what she had done for herself. If Mo had, at last, recognized the existence of the forest as something other than an environment to be measured, she had not yet come to an understanding of it that the forest recognized as itself.

The eye of the forest observed Mo observing it and mistaking it, and reached out wordlessly to that part of her that was deaf to everything but words. And Mo, in her sleep, tangled in the forest, sensed something, though she understood nothing. She was touched – irrationally, as it would seem to her – as she had been touched before by feelings that made no sense whatever once she woke.

So the forest in Mo lay dormant as she went about her busy life, and waited, not understanding her, for her to understand it. Mo woke in the morning, early, with the dawn chorus of gibbon cries, the unearthly howls that ushered in their day and hers, and rang around the high canopy like a coronet of sound. An image of Joe, naked and muscular, lay on her eyelids and she recalled the duet she had played with the forest the night before. She blinked the image away, ashamed and embarrassed that she had indulged such foolish fantasies. The sounds of the forest were out there in the bright clearing, just the noises of the world she studied, not actually related to her or her body, which, fresh and rested, threw off the sleeping bag and the memory of the previous night, and prepared for a busy day ahead.

She climbed into her still-damp working jeans and shirt and prepared breakfast, fully herself again. She was who she was, the world was outside, external now in the clear light of day. And last night was the past, already forgotten. But still, as she stepped out of her tent into the tiny clearing and looked at the trees soaring above her on all sides, there was a curious image, a harshness, a sort of triumph about them. Nonsense, she said aloud, as she strode into the forest, her rucksack on her back, towards her ground plan of squares.

Fourteen

Mo had been working for most of the morning checking the growth quadrats at Site One. She knelt in the centre of square 6H measuring the diameter of a half-grown tree that had been colonized by a strangling ficus. Then she checked the length of the strangler's aerial roots that had begun to surround the tree and head for the ground. Eventually, when enough of its roots had embedded themselves in the soil, the ficus would be self-supporting, ready to grow up to the light from its stilted advantage, and the host tree would die, its own roots suffocated by the uninvited guest. She jotted the results in the notebook that lay on the ground beside her.

She was being watched.

As ever, she was observed by the composite vision of the forest, by the doomed tree and the strangling fig; by the millipedes which had been diverted by the weight and substance of her khaki-covered knee pressing on the earth; by the still, glossy leaves of the lower canopy above her head that sensed and adjusted for the increased CO_2 levels she caused. But as well as being subject to the continual unintentioned monitoring of the forest, she was also *watched*. That is, a pair of eyes actively focused on Mo, and far from being the neutral stare that the forest, had it eyes, would have given her, these eyes, a cool azure that was to be seen nowhere else in this environment, these eyes glistened with amusement and narrowed, the brows above them raised slightly in humour and judgement.

They saw Mo surrounded by acres of forest, on her knees in the middle of a marked out plot almost central in a system of squares, gently brushing away a patch of soil with her fingers. She was searching for any new shoots ready to emerge, so that she could mark them out on her plan. Her hair was pulled back with a slide and a band of material circled her brow to keep the sweat from running into her eyes as she worked. She wore a grey checked cotton skirt tucked into loose army surplus trousers that were themselves tucked into strong jungle boots, designed to keep out biting insects and leeches. The eyes watched as she scraped at the earth with her fingertips, occasionally picking up a tiny piece of debris and putting it to one side carefully, so that she could return it once her investigation was over.

Below the eyes, a mouth curled into a smile.

'I see you're still tidying up. If I'd known, I'd have brought a dustpan and brush for you. But I've got some salt in my back pack if wine's the problem.'

Mo brought her head up sharply and sat back on her heels as she searched the half-light for the source of the voice. She recognized the words instantly, but her eyes could only make out a hazily human-shaped shadow some ten metres away, concealed by a latticework of ferns and leafy branches. She remained where she was squinting into the distance, refusing to acknowledge what she knew until her eyes confirmed it.

Joe pushed the branches aside and strode up to the edge of the gridded area, undeniably himself.

'Hello,' he smiled. Mo stood up, but stayed where she was inside her square.

'Joe?' she asked, as if there was still a remote possibility that it was not. His head dipped in assent and the lips curved again into their familiar mixture of scorn and humour.

'You mean you weren't expecting me? Don't move.' A blinding flash of white light illuminated the grid for a second. 'You can call this one "Mo clearing up the jungle".' He pulled the blank photograph from the Polaroid camera and held it dangling by one corner, ignoring the image that began to emerge. Mo's eyes took a moment to readjust to the gloom.

'What are you doing here?'

'Thought I'd drop by and pay you a visit. See how you were

getting on. I didn't have any special plans for the summer vacation, so I thought I'd do a little travelling. I pointed my compass east, and you were more or less en route.'

Mo stepped carefully across the five 1.5 metre plots to the edge of the grid. She pulled off her headband and wiped the sweat from her face with it.

'But how did you get here?'

'Same way as you. I checked your exact location with Sally in the office, got to the research station, and Leloh was kind enough to lend me his longboat and point me in the right direction. He seemed pleased that you were going to have a visitor. Says it's bad for women to spend too much time alone in the forest. Aren't you going to offer me a cup of tea?'

Mo continued to stand and stare for a moment.

'This is ridiculous. Completely ridiculous. You've no right to. . .'

She stopped, hearing the echo of a previous conversation that she had not come out of well. She rubbed the soil from her hands. 'We'd better go back to the clearing,' she said briskly, packing her stuff away into the rucksack. 'This way.'

Joe raised his hand in mock salute and they marched back along Mo's path in silent single file.

In the tent Joe shrugged his rucksack off his shoulders and let it lay where it dropped. He flung himself on to the camp bed with a groan. 'God, I'm exhausted. I'd forgotten what this climate was like.'

Mo lit the camping stove and put some water on to boil. 'It can be very dangerous if you're not used to it. I suppose you know that, though,' she added, remembering this was not his first visit to a tropical forest. She turned round to ask him what he had come for.

Joe was already asleep.

Mo released the mosquito netting and let it fall around him like a shroud. She finished making tea and when it had brewed sat in the canvas chair at her desk watching her sleeping visitor.

Perhaps, she thought, I'm seeing things. Perhaps the jungle has got to me. But she knew he was real, lying there in his sweat-stained olive-greens, his arms flung back beside his head on the pillow. He was very substantial. *There*. She did not know why though, what he wanted. If her father were alive, he would have come to visit, but that would have been understandable – intellectual curiosity. Perhaps that was why Joe was here, but she knew that wasn't *all*. There had to be something else.

Joe's slightly fevered dream seeped into the forest. The real forest outside the tent absorbed his nightmare memories of another forest, far away in space and time. It took in his human images of marginal life and pointless death and recoiled from the human memory of human suffering. Screaming mouths, fearful eyes, the accumulated hopelessness of years of struggle to keep a child fed, and then to watch it wiped away in a fireball that was meant for anyone. The forest took in the human need for purpose, a point to life and death, and the desolation of the creature that discovered there was none, and it could not understand such pain at all. The images in Joe's dream were nothing but confusion to the forest which knew nothing of suffering, or purpose, and so just was, or was not. It turned its gaze away and simply continued, as Joe had tried to do. But Joe, being human and having nowhere else to gaze, had confused detachment with indifference, and so stood apart from everything.

Three hours later Mo was bent over her desk working, when Joe woke. He stretched and yawned. 'This is a hell of a place for dreaming. Don't ask.' He extended his arm beyond the stretch towards Mo. 'Come here,' he said quietly. 'I want to fuck you in your jungle.'

And once he had said it, it seemed to Mo there was no question that he would. Perhaps he was right, she wondered, perhaps she had been expecting him.

She raised the netting and sat straight, not looking at him, on the edge of the bed, while he manoevered his clothes off without getting up. Then he undressed Mo who remained still as he undid buttons, unlaced boots, lifted her slightly to slide off her trousers, and, when she was naked, patted the space on the bed beside him, directing her to lie down.

For a few moments they lay in silence, side by side, listening to the clicks and chatter of the forest. Then Joe turned towards her and began to trace the contours of her body with his index finger, very delicately, starting at her neck and moving down, sketching her shape with the tip of his finger that slid lightly over her moist, sweaty skin. It moved slowly up and then down one breast, across the parallel lines of her ribs and over the slight swell of her stomach, pausing for a moment at the depression of her navel. Then down again, to draw the angle of her crotch and to run along the line of her closed inner thighs; to knee, to calf, finally coming to rest on her ankle, where his other fingers extended and enclosed her in an increasingly tightening grip.

'Remember me?' he asked after he had slid his hand smoothly back by the same route to rest lightly around her neck.

Mo and the forest remembered her need. Once she had turned the forest into her lover. Now, the throb of the forest beat strongly, and he was here, his hand, as real as the sounds outside the tent, stroking and playing on her body in time to a rhythm she could no longer place. His, her's, or the forest's – it didn't matter.

They made love for a long afternoon, their bodies, saturated with exertion and the heat, slipping against each other. Joe's practised hands and body orchestrated her, increasing her need, sustaining it and fulfilling it, like a composer writing down the notes he had already in his inner ear, until Mo felt a rhythm of her own, and began to weave her own melody with her hands and mouth and pelvis so that it became another fugue, like the one she had played with the forest. A pattern of opposing, but coterminous rhythms.

They lay quietly afterwards listening to the evening storm rumbling in the distance, making its way towards them. When the thunder broke with an ear-splitting crack over their heads and the first huge drops of rain fell, Joe got up.

'Being a clean and wholesome lad, I'm going to have a wash.'

He left the tent and stood naked in the clearing amid the downpour, letting the rain beat on his body, raising his arms to allow it to flow down them, turning this way and that, running his hands through his dripping hair, rubbing himself all over with his flattened palms. The force that sustained the forest became his private shower and he hugely enjoyed the joke. He matched the energy of the storm with his own, making a washroom facility of the deluge that elsewhere tore up hundred-foot trees that had stood for centuries, drowned living things too small or slow to escape, and gave life to the forest in spite of that. Mo got up from the bed to see what he was doing and stood naked just inside the threshold of the tent watching his parody. She enjoyed the joke too, and smiled, but was uneasily aware of the contempt that underlay his game. It was all game to him, everything. What mattered enough to be taken seriously? She pushed the thought away, wanting the enjoyment as he called to her to join him. Sticky with sweat and sex, she stepped out into the storm-drenched clearing, into his beckoning arms. He rinsed her down in the rain that fell as if from great gutters in the sky, swivelling and pivoting her around to get to every part of her body. The rain streamed into her face from the hair plastered to her head by the weight of falling water, so that she could barely see him laughing and spluttering away the rain that ran into his mouth. Mo laughed with him and tried to stroke the wetness from his face. It was extraordinary and wonderful to be standing naked in the open clearing in the forest, washing in a storm.

It was as near as she had ever been to allowing the forest to be part of her – being with it, using it, and feeling its force on her. She neither observed it or herself and was, momentarily, content to be there with her lover, with whom the act of sex became a discovery of pleasure and ease with herself. She felt lovely, and her strong practical limbs moved with a new grace that must always have been there waiting for permission. Joe began to sing a bathroom medley in a strong tenor voice and she danced with him in the storm like one who had just invented this new and completely pointless activity for her body. It was no longer constrained by purpose: walking to get to . . . sitting in order that . . . It moved for its own pleasure in ways that practical activity would never require and was delighted at its capacity for beauty.

When the storm had passed they rubbed each other dry, shivering and laughing, inside the tent and put on clean clothes. Mo set about preparing a meal while Joe sat on the bed beside her and rested his arm around her shoulder, stroking her cheek absent-mindedly from time to time. She squatted on the floor and watched the rice dancing in the bubbling water on the stove, feeling exhausted, in a slow motion of well-being. She was a stone carving whose outside was being worn away and coming ever closer to what it really was as the effects of time and weather rubbed out the form imposed by chisel and the image in some other mind's eye. Inside the created image was a true form that was the stone itself. She had a sense that her edges were being rubbed away, and, for the first time, that the external form was not perhaps the essence, that there was a glowing place in her that could be allowed to grow. She experienced this place physically as somewhere beneath the knot of anger, the fist in her that tightened when she read her mother's letter, or thought of Liam's foolishness. Beneath there, geographically, was something that wanted to exist. Mo and the forest were suddenly very close. The queen termite whispered of necessity, and the creepers, still saturated and dripping, rustled patterns of connection at Mo from their place below the clenched fist, and out there in the forest. And Mo almost heard them as she listened to the hiss of the gas from the cooker. She knew, at least, that there was something she needed to hear.

She was disoriented by the day's events. Solid, sensible Mo felt that her bearings had shifted and that she floated in a no-man's-land, away from herself. Not herself, not anything. Her work in the forest no longer seemed precisely central. It seemed that there might be a new task at hand; some memories she had to have, some connection she must make in order to feel inside herself again. But she was not, at the moment, sure what that self was. She knew that the Mo she had left behind at her grid this morning – slipped out of as a snake slides away from its outgrown skin – would hold her in contempt. Just a fuss about sex. That's all it was. She could hear herself, but distantly, beyond the path she had made through the forest to her grid. Well, it was true. She could not think of any other way to describe it. Need. Wanting. His powerful physical presence, and the fact that when they made love, he had *fitted* her, not just in the obvious way, but all of him, so that being close was like finding another part of herself she had not even known she had lost.

Naturally the Mo of the grids would disapprove. It made no sense. Wasn't sensible. But the Mo who had lost her bearings knew something the other didn't about necessity. It crossed her mind that perhaps tomorrow she would re-read Marjorie's letter, and that Liam deserved, if not her sympathy, at least more attention to what he was saying. Perhaps sometimes you have to take what you want, and the untidy consequences along with it. But what about other people, what about the carefully constructed edifices, the coherence of things? Why was Liam wilfully pulling everything down around his ears? In that situation everyone was hurt. How could that be acceptable? She saw in the bubbling rice a tableaux of the sitting room in Sussex. John, Marjorie and Mo sitting in the silence of the ticking clock; a frozen image of family. What would have been the consequences, if each of them had taken what they wanted, on that still image? Hadn't they all survived their unachieved longings? But now she was not sure what it was that either of her parents *had* wanted. She knew she had never considered them outside their relationship with her. They had been two converging lines whose meeting point was herself, the crucial angle. Now it seemed that there had been three separate lines, none straight, all entangled at certain points, but each having a direction of its own. She sifted through the anger, irritation and longing of her childhood and knew that what she had wanted – that she still could not quite name – would have brought the tenuous structure of her family tumbling to the ground. Everyone would have lost everything in the resulting mess. If she hadn't precisely identified the danger as a child, she had known it was there, and constructed a protective scaffolding that had somehow become the thing itself. Without its scrupulous pattern everything was in danger of crumbling. She thought she had been enabling everything to go on safely, but perhaps that was not so, and it seemed to her now that she had built the scaffolding around herself and that it was not, as she had thought, for the protection of others.

'Let's eat,' Joe interrupted, and Mo's tentative musings faded as the present demanded her attention. She dished up the rice and handed him his bowl, and they chatted quietly about what had been going on at college and how the course Joe had taught had gone. And next year, in September, when Mo returned to London? Joe shrugged. He put his empty bowl on the crate beside the bed.

'I'm going for a walk,' he said suddenly, and was gone for the best part of two hours. Mo decided not to worry about him, remembering he was familiar with rainforest.

He returned looking exhausted and drawn, but managed a vague smile. 'Let's go to bed. You've got a busy day at the grids tomorrow.'

In spite of his lightness of tone Joe made angry love to Mo. He moved inside her urgently, and she saw in his eyes only a blue reflection of her own anxious face. Mo held him, but he was not with her. He went through her towards his orgasm and immediate sleep. She lay beside him on the narrow bed and listened to the croaking of the frogs and the buzzing of the insects. The forest outside seemed suddenly threatening and disorderly. She could feel it pulling at her flesh as if it could not bear the contained boundaries of her body and were trying to find a way to unravel her. She looked at Joe sleeping and wondered what he dreamed about.

In the morning after breakfast Mo pulled out her charts and diagrams from the box beside her desk. Joe had woken late and seemed in good enough humour.

'Let me show you what I've been doing, then the grid sites will make more sense when you see them.'

Joe got up from the bed and stood beside Mo's chair, one arm resting on the edge of the desk, as Mo began to explain the way the data had been transferred to paper. She finished explaining one diagram and was about to pull another roll of paper from the box when Joe interrupted. 'Well, it all looks fine. You've been working away like a beaver.' He moved away from the table and began to put things into his rucksack.

'But I haven't finished showing you,' Mo began. 'You won't make head or tail of the grids unless you see the growth patterns.'

'I'm not as interested as you in forest ecology,' he said, still putting things away. 'I don't care very much. Anyway, I won't be able to visit your site. I've got to get back.'

'Get back?' Mo didn't understand what he meant. 'I thought you'd be staying for a few days. Where do you have to get back to?'

'No, I just dropped by to say hello.' He pulled the cord tight around the opening of the rucksack. 'We're on our way to Sydney.'

'We?' Mo asked, knowing what was coming.

'I'm travelling with Mariana. You remember, she was doing her post-grad in the anthropology department. I left her back at the research station, pumping Derek for his Australian contacts. I may stay out there for a while. I don't know.'

He eyed her coolly. His tone suggested that this last piece of information had just slipped his mind earlier. It was of no great importance.

Mo got up from the desk. 'And yesterday, last night. . . ?'

'Was fun. Wasn't it? I had a really nice time, Mo. I'm glad I came out to see you. Anyway, you wouldn't want me around distracting you from your work.'

'Why didn't you tell me?'

'Tell you what? I didn't lie to you. We're both grown-ups, Mo. We fucked and it was good. That's all. There's no problem.' This last was insistent, final. He swung his rucksack on to his back. 'I'll be off down-river. There's one thing that occurred to me though, about your grids and your search for the ultimate truth about rainforests. Supposing they're in the wrong place, your squares? Supposing they're in the one place that *doesn't* give you a representative sample of the whole forest? Supposing,' he continued with a sudden laugh as the thought came to him, 'the truth you're searching for is *between* your squares, or concealed by the lines that make the framework of the grid? All those bits of paper would be meaningless, wouldn't they?' He crossed the tent and kissed Mo on the cheek, then stepped back and looked carefully at her stunned, impassive face. 'It's OK. I was only joking. Take care. See you.' And he left through the opening of the tent with a wave of the back of his hand.

Mo began to change from her dry night kit into the damp working outfit and pulled on her other practical, protective layers as she dressed. A connection she had once made in her mind now returned and locked tight. Joe and the forest. They were the same. Both dangerous, beguiling the unwary into forgetting to be watchful. Each hid cruel and sudden surprises. Mo knew she survived the real dangers of the forest because she took care not to assume that things were as they seemed.

Snakes and poisonous insects; leeches and fever; accident, infection, disorientation. They lurked, waiting for the carelessness of the unwatchful. She survived the forest by knowing it, by testing and looking and breaking it down into separate compartments. It was never to be trusted. Once out of one's control anything could happen. The correspondence between Joe and the forest was irresistible. Both destructive, both uncaring. She pulled the laces of her boots tightly over her trousers and remembered where and who she was. She was, she thought, back in her work clothes, back in her proper self. Mo the scientist, the Mo of the grids. Three squares at Grid Two remained unchecked from yesterday. Her efficient schedule had been disrupted. Now she must get back to the real task.

She was, in fact, as far as she had ever been from the objective, data-gathering scientist. She had created a new forest out of her own turmoil; given it a face, a name, and a quality that matched not the reality of the forest, but the personal chaos that threatened to engulf her.

The forest could no longer find a space in Mo in which it could exist. The place it had inhabited, small and unrecognized as it was, contracted now to nothing. Sometimes in the forest there were creatures that grew wrong, by birth or accident, that never connected with the ordinary cycles of life, and so were unable to sustain themselves. They were recognizable always by their blankness, their inability to reflect back at the life that extended towards them. They expired as aliens; picked off too easily by predators who knew them by the illuminating pool of darkness surrounding them; or killed by their own kind, disturbed at the emptiness they encountered. While they lived, the forest maintained a vigil, watched the life that should have been of it, but could never be. It perceived and noted the wrongness and waited for the death that would reintegrate them when their substance leeched into the soil and was transformed into new and effective life.

The forest withdrew from Mo and watched.

Mo pulled on her rucksack full of notebooks and pushed her hair under her floppy canvas hat. She didn't care. There was no place in her that cared or wanted anything at all. Except to get on with her work. Nothing hurt; she felt tight and strong.

Leloh wasn't coming to pick her up for three days and she supposed Joe and his friend would have left the research station by then. She would not permit the last day to be anything more than an unnecessary interruption of her schedule.

Striding along her private path to Grid One, she shouldered past the giant palm leaves and sharp ferns that encroached, already threatening to block her way. Today the rucksack seemed heavier than usual and by the time she neared the grid site, her breathing was laboured. The soaking air and unrelenting heat were taking more out of her than usual. She inhaled deeply, trying for more air and her breathing rate accelerated. Every now and again she stopped for a moment and wiped the sweat from her face with the back of her shirtsleeve. She felt she was being watched, but looking round saw and heard nothing out of the ordinary, and carried on until she arrived at her site, knowing that even after several months this climate could get to be too much sometimes. She dropped her rucksack from her shoulders and squatted for a moment on the ground at the edge of the grid, trying to get her breath back.

The sense of being watched came again as she sat there, sorting out her notebooks. She felt eyes peering at her and her pulse and respiration began to race again as she stared around at the empty forest. Confused, she looked about her, suddenly no longer sure if she were observing or being observed. She knew there was no person there, but still, her own watching seemed reflected back at her.

She was watched. She was certain; didn't know what was happening. She was there to look and understand the forest that was external and passive, but now she herself was subject to an observation as clinical and detached as her own. Or so it seemed. For a moment the boundary between herself and the forest was at risk, but she fought through that, refusing to allow in the fear that crept around her. It was like the humidity, that fear, mingled inseparably with the breathable oxygen, so that it was as difficult to keep out. She breathed carefully as if the right kind of inhalation, shallow, concentrated, would filter the oxygen into her lungs, leaving the moisture and fear behind.

As she stood up and walked over to the grid a pressure in her began to rise from low in her abdomen, like a pair of hands squeezing tight. Up; pressing on her rib cage, and to her chest where they gripped harder compressing her lungs. And then to her head; her skull encased in a steel cage, being crushed, outside and then inside, pressing on her brain; the tension concentrated now on squeezing the soft matter of her mind to a pulp.

She stood very still, trying to separate the buzzing of the forest in her ears from the buzzing pressure in her head. 'No,' she said aloud, stating it. 'This won't happen. I won't let this happen, whatever it is. I'm all right. I'm all right.' The pressure seemed to lessen as she spoke and she took long, deep breaths.

Suddenly she was no longer quite inside herself. The tension in her head had gone, but it was as if some damage had been done, and whatever it was that anchored her consciousness to her body had almost, but not quite, been cut through. At any moment, she knew, her mind would fly off, separate from her, and only an act of will kept it from happening. Things became hazy and she pulled herself back, trying to remake the reality that was slipping away. She was in a state of terror, convinced that once she lost control and allowed her mind to float away she would never get back to the solid vision that connected her with the real world that she had never before had cause to doubt. She saw the external orderly world around her flying off, falling to pieces, disintegrating, and all the order she had always known the world to be threaten to break down, to become a meaningless mass of swirling particles. It was no metaphorical vision, this; she was seeing it, her brain suddenly the enemy of organized pattern; her own enemy.

She held on desperately to what she knew of reality, and the final separation she feared did not quite happen, not entirely. The threat of chaos hovered over her and at the periphery of her vision, but didn't quite take over. She would not allow it, but knew she could not relax for a second. She had to continue as if everything were normal, attempting to push herself back inside her head by getting on with things as though nothing out of the ordinary were happening.

Mo looked at her notebook and then at the grid, trying to remember which squares were due for checking. It seemed, although she was standing by the very edge of it, as if she were looking down the wrong end of a telescope. The whole grid was far away and diminished by distance.

It was quadrat 4D today, she decided, and made her legs move across the grid towards it. Then she stopped as a thought came into her mind. Perhaps Joe was right. What if she had placed the grids wrongly? It was possible, wasn't it, that she had chosen too particular a piece of land to study? What if, by accident, these squares were not quite like the rest of the forest? How was she to know? And if that were so, what of her findings? They would be invalid. Wrong. All the charts, the diagrams, the accumulated data – useless. She would just be measuring a particular, special patch of ground that told her nothing about the overall pattern of the forest. If a random sample turned out not to be random at all, not a sample . . . How was one to know? More studies, more grids, control grids. She only had two sites and she couldn't know if either was truly representative, or how one should judge.

These thoughts took place slightly above her head, as she stared at the pattern of squares through eyes that felt remote, as if sight beamed out of them rather than light rays beaming in to her optic nerve and to her brain. Thought and behaviour were no longer exactly synchronized. Her body did as she instructed, but at a remove, a machine that was controlled from only the slightest distance but that made all the difference in the world. She breathed carefully, putting the thoughts into action and relaying the information from her body back to her mind. Trying to maintain a semblance of normality was a massive effort, took all her attention, but she feared even a fraction of a second's lapse of concentration. She would be lost. Everything was put into control and normality. There was nothing left over for judgement; for observing the quality of her own thoughts.

What was wrong was that the grids were not in the right place. This was clear to her now. And that she could do something about. It might be only a matter of inches, she thought. The real sample just out of kilter with her imposed boundaries. Perhaps the proper squares were half in one, half in the next. Or something like that. How could she be sure? How would she tell when they were right?

Mo began to get a sharp pain in her head and directed her body to move. She pulled up the nearest peg holding down the nylon string that marked the boundaries of the squares. Then another, and another. She would remake the site, mark out different squares, half a metre down from her original framework.

She spent half the morning pulling up pegs, winding string and replacing everything in its new position. When she finished she stood, her body and mind frantic, racing, at one end of the grid and looked at it. Was it right? She was worried about the string and the wooden pegs. What if they themselves spoiled the sample? String was narrow, it was true, but what of the accumulated area the string covered? All the string, bounding all the squares, would add up to a substantial amount of territory. A notional line had no thickness. Not so half a mile of string. She had a calculator in her rucksack. There were – she punched the buttons – 135 metres of string altogether in her ten 1.5 metre squares. If the string was, say, 3 millimetres thick, that would mean – she punched more buttons – more than 1 square metre of ground that couldn't be studied because it was covered with string. That would put her figures out completely. Wouldn't it? She wasn't sure if she was right. If the problem she had just worked out was the real problem.

She buried her face in her hands for a moment, pressing her fingers tight against her skull, trying to think straight.

It was the sampling that was the problem, not the string. She could only know if she had a truly representative site if she had more than two grids on separated sites. How many more than two, she wondered? How many would be enough? She didn't have enough string with her, it was back at the clearing, and where should she place the new grids? Two of them, equidistant, in opposite directions from the existing ones, she decided. She felt everything slipping away. Had to make a decision. She packed her rucksack and made for the clearing.

Mo struggled back along her path concentrating hard on the reality around her. She made a mental picture of herself walking through the forest, herself and her surroundings, practical facts, but the mental picture only seemed to confirm her distance from the world. Her mind, like a balloon filled with helium, was lighter than air, and pulling away, trying to release itself to fly up and out of reach. She held on to it as it tried to tug free, a child holding the string of a balloon and feeling it jerk wilfully, dangerously powerful. And her heart raced, thumping in her chest until it felt her whole body was beating, she could feel its insistent rhythm pounding every part of her as if it too were trying to break out. For a second she wondered if she weren't having a heart attack; perhaps she was dying. She was sure she was dying. But that didn't seem as dangerous as literally losing her mind and never getting back inside herself.

Once she was at the clearing the extraordinary difficulty of what she intended to do struck her. *To make two more 15 metre grids.* Getting back, then to the new site, two of them, then marking, aligning and setting out the string. It had taken her days to complete the original sites and then she was fresh and not so . . . confused. She became dizzy with the time, the effort, the impossibility of what she was doing.

The forest watched, and would have held its breath had it been human. As it was birds called and cried, monkeys screeched, insects clicked, leaves sweated and dripped more moisture into the atmosphere. Everything continued as it had to, and the chaos that was Mo stood still in the clearing and shook with the terror of disintegration. She trembled from the very core so that it seemed her bones quaked, and deep, explosive sobs shuddered through her body until her own sounds drowned out the noise of the forest. Mo sank to her knees at the threshold of her tent and sobbed in terror as she watched the world around her break up into infinitely small particles, whirling and circling between the shafts of light. Closing in on her, moving towards her until her own boundaries were breached and she herself became a mass of disorganized matter and there was no longer any difference between here and there.

Fifteen

Leloh found her two days later when he arrived to pick her up. She lay on the ground just inside the tent, curled up, very still, her eyes open, unblinking. For a moment he thought she was dead, but when he pushed her filthy, matted hair off her face, the skin was warm and he felt a pulse beating in her neck. Her face was smeared with dirt, soil from the forest floor, caked and muddied by moisture, rain or tears. She showed no signs of recognition, or of life beyond her blood heat and the circulation through her veins. Leloh had seen distraction before in people and in animals. It happened sometimes, he knew. He got her on to the bed and then went back to the research station for help. Someone radioed for a helicopter while Derek and another man went with Leloh to bring Mo back to Base Camp.

Back in London, in the hospital, Mo sat in her small, white-walled side room off the main ward. To an observer, looking through the six-inch-square window in the top of the door, she appeared peaceful, sitting on the chair beside the bed, her hands folded quietly in her lap. Her clean, well-brushed hair fell neatly to her shoulders and her eyes were shut. But she was not asleep. She had discovered that it made no difference whether they were open or closed. She still saw what she saw.

The walls ran sweat. Rivulets of water streamed unendingly, soaking the high gloss paint so that it cracked and broke up, falling away to reveal the reality beneath. The room was saturated with moisture and heat; the water ran, the air was still, hot and wet. It was like trying to breathe through a towel soaked in bath water. Shafts of sunlight broke up the surfaces of the walls and exposed an impossible tangle of growth; creepers, thorns, a dozen different shapes of leaves pushing and twisting through each other to gain space. The living and dead detritus of an environment grown rampant beyond its capacity and strangling itself and everything in it with the inescapable, deadly ropes of excess life. Much more terrible, more final than death, which seemed to Mo to be a clean, white, finite place of repose. A place she could reach. Death, she told herself, imagining a safe haven from the dreadful forces of life that suffocated and strangled her, was a white room with four high, brittle, glossy white walls, meeting with absolute inevitability at four absolute ninety-degree angles. No matter how thin you made yourself, she thought, you could never slip through the place where the walls met. Lines do not meet at infinity, they meet at the corners of rooms and create the finite safety of a dead end.

But she could not get to the room. She existed inside a fetid chaos of jungle. A soaking, stench-filled labyrinth with no centre, where even the air threatened to drown you. Everything in the deep green gloom was arbitrary, pointless, random. An accidental hell that would grow until the life was squeezed out of everything. Chaotic, disordered, wild with undisciplined, unstoppable growth. The millions of separate bits made no coherent pattern, and denied all hope of sense.

Mo sat with her eyes closed, imprisoned in her vision of hell. Although the rainforest had left her, unable to maintain its link, she now inhabited a forest of her own creation. She sat within it, in the small, white room, very still, trying with every cell of herself to stay separate and safe from the engulfing danger. Somewhere, in the far distance, there were people's voices, she heard her name, a door opening and closing, footsteps. But all that was very remote, much too far away for her to make herself heard, to have any hope of rescue. She tried not to think about time, because that made the terror of being forever stuck in this dreadful place threaten to expand and take her over completely. Then she would be finally lost. She must simply sit still and not think about anything at all.

Once or twice she thought she heard her mother's voice, but she knew she imagined it. Her mother, she was certain, was in the house in Sussex, doing something to the garden. She couldn't possibly survive in a jungle. And her father? Where was he? She half expected him to come and get her out of this terrible place, but then she remembered. He would be with Sheila, or someone, or somewhere. He wouldn't have the time to come and find her. Too busy. Somewhere else.

Then gradually the forest began to fade slightly, and the hazy outlines of a room started to appear, uncertainly at first, but then more strongly as the drug she was receiving began to take effect. Quite soon, the fearsome forest was gone, and she was firmly, solidly, in a small square room, with glossy white walls.

Sixteen

Marjorie stood against the dark Victorian brick wall of the play-ground, bent over a grazed and bleeding knee.

'It's not too bad,' she soothed, 'I think it looks worse than it really is. You go in to the nurse and get it cleaned up. Then come back and show me your plaster.'

The small boy limped into the school, hiccuping away his sobs dramatically. Marjorie picked up her mug of tea from the window ledge and drank from it as her eyes wandered about the busy playground.

Fifty small children made frantic patterns on the dark tarmac: a dozen little groups, jumping, running and squatting, with occasional runners, making connections or rearrangements between the groups, weaving in and out of the spaces between the sets. The noise, if you permitted your ears to listen at that pitch, was deafening, painful. Squealing, shrieking, occasionally a full-throated scream for the sheer pleasure of making a tremendous sound, free from the constraints of teacher and classroom.

Marjorie had been working here as a playground helper for almost a year now; long enough to perceive the patterns beneath the ex-traordinary disorder that would have struck an adult stranger suddenly arriving in the middle of infants' playtime. She watched the flashing comings and goings of love and friendship; the tests and trials; betrayals, despair and new pairings formed, all within the space of the fifteen-minute first playtime of the day. Later, she knew, during lunch and afternoon play, all these dramas would be re-enacted. By the end of the day nothing very much would have been altered, or not finally anyway.

Tina walked, as usual, around the perimeter of the playground, her small body pressed tight against the walls. She would eventually arrive at Marjorie, and it would be time for a chat and a cuddle.

'Hello, Tina.'

'Can I take your cup in, Miss?'

'Soon. I'm not quite finished. How are you today?'

''Right, Miss. I hate this school. No one likes me.' The voice dull, accepting. These were the facts of life. And they were. Tina had arrived a year and a term after most of the other children in her class, who had by then sorted out their positions. They did not like Tina, not because she was black: so were many of them; nor because she had no dad: that was true of a good proportion of the others too; but because she had arrived late and was shy. Tina had known before she entered the school gate for the first time that no one would like her, and the other children knew as soon as she entered that they didn't. So she spent her playtimes walking around the edge of the playground in her quiet, accepting way.

'I like your shoes, Tina. Are they new?'

'Yes, Miss. They won't play with me, Miss, not even if I asked,' Tina said firmly, forestalling any suggestion Marjorie might attempt. But Marjorie had seen by now the truth of what Tina said.

'Well, you stay here with me, and then you can take my cup in. I think,' she said, very hesitantly, 'that it will be all right if you give it a bit more time.'

She was not certain it would, but thought it might. She wanted very much to help Tina through the pain of being alone and rejected, wanted to comfort her, but over the weeks had understood that she could not make light of what was happening. They both knew that this was how things were and Tina was not to be comforted with a pretence, she had made that clear. So Marjorie gave her a hug and told her about Sussex and her garden, the seeds she had sown, the birds that would come and nest, the way things grew in clumps that got wider and broader over the seasons so that eventually there would be a patchwork of colour covering the back of the garden.

*

It had happened almost by accident. One day, shortly after Mo left for the rainforest, Marjorie had gone up to London to do some shopping. Afterwards, amid the confusing crowds of tourists and lunchtime shoppers in Oxford Street, she remembered she had the key to Mo's flat in her handbag, for safekeeping. She sat wearily on the top deck of the bus heading for Kentish Town, gazing down at the bustle and the tops of people's heads, thinking again how distant she had always been from the frantic rush that was going on below and around her. She watched harassed faces coming into view and then disappearing as the bus made its way north. Women with small children boarded with two or three bags, trying to steady themselves and their children and get seated before the bus jerked away from the stop. They snapped angrily at the fidgeting children who whined with the boredom and discomfort of it all.

The city seemed to Marjorie an awful trial; even people who were not cross and struggling had a look of determination about them that made her feel tired and weak.

It was not like this in Sussex. And life had always been Sussex, she realized. She had a picture, as she sat sipping tea in Mo's flat, of London as a vast network of individual lives, each crossing and re-crossing others, but with no defined end, no final purpose, all getting on with their own necessities. It was like a particularly complex version of the underground map, itself something she had not quite got to the bottom of. Dozens of lines intersecting and cutting across each other, but ending nowhere in particular, just stopping at the end of the line, at the edge of the diagram. Millions of individuals, feeling themselves individual, living and growing, making an accidental pattern that created the city. It seemed strange to her, now, that for years she had come here; popped in, shopped, or gone to the theatre, and then left, without a thought for what kind of place she was in, without any curiosity.

She decided to stay a few days, and walked around, watching and listening, riding buses that took her to parts of the city she had never even heard of. Mostly it was grey and dilapidated, but she began to notice curtains, colours of front doors, patches of front gardens declaring a personal interest among the uniform dullness of the brick and paving. She left the flat early and returned home after dark, perceiving the patterns of the day: children going to school, men and women at work, pushchairs and bags for shopping, the suddenly crowded bus as school finished and then later, when work was over and people headed home. Like her, not everyone had a destination. She began to recognize the different look of the elderly and the unemployed who made their journeys without being on their way to somewhere. And she talked to people. Conversations began easily: the weather, the time it took for a bus to come, a girl across the street with an outrageous hairstyle. They continued if encouraged, to tell or complain of their lives, families, neighbours, the state of the world. A ready fund of opinion and information, waiting only for someone to show an interest. One woman was on her way home from her job as a non-teaching helper in a primary school. Marjorie had not known that such a job existed and asked about it. It seemed she was as qualified as anyone else, and the next morning she walked to the primary school near Mo's flat. They did need someone to help out for three days a week and, after an interview, Marjorie was given the job almost before she realized that she was asking for it.

Back in Sussex, excited and scared, she half feared that once she got inside the house she would call the school and tell them she could not manage after all. She had no idea if she could cope, if she could do what was needed, or indeed what *was* needed. She hadn't had a job before. But she did not make the call and began, instead, to think about how to break the news to Mo. She did not know why she put it like this to herself, or why she decided to wait until Mo returned from the forest. She would simply tell Mo that she was using the flat occasionally, and explain what had happened when she got back. There was plenty of time to find herself a room to rent nearby.

But before the term began Mo got ill and was sent home to the hospital.

Marjorie stayed in Mo's flat and made daily visits to Mo. It was a shock, at first, seeing her competent daughter so – blank. The doctors said the strain of living alone in the forest, the climate, and her particularly rigid personality had combined to cause the breakdown, but that with the help of drugs and plenty of rest they were sure she would make a good recovery.

For two weeks Marjorie visited but could do nothing more than sit and hold her absent daughter's hand. She seemed quite lost. Sometimes Marjorie talked quietly about the house and what was happening in the village, but there was no response. She felt terribly sad for Mo, so unreachable. But this was not a new feeling, just more extreme. If her daughter was a stranger, she was only *more* of a stranger. She loved Mo, cared about her, and, of course, wanted her to get better, but she saw, during that time, that Mo had always been very distant. Always. And the ache Marjorie felt for her now was something she had lived with for as long as she could remember. She wished that things had been different; if the three of them had been different. But Mo was now an adult. Marjorie might mourn the distant child Mo had been, but she had to accept the adult for what she was.

She sat in the room waiting for Mo's nightmare to finish, knowing that when it did they would still be separate people; concerned, involved, but not tied together in a close emotional bond. They were two adults, each conducting their own lives, entitled and obliged to do so. She could not and would not expect Mo to become someone she wasn't; and she also, she knew, had to get on with what she was.

Marjorie understood this sitting in the white hospital room. Mistakes had been made, she knew. It was sad, but it was so.

As Mo improved and began to think about leaving the hospital, it was agreed that Marjorie should take over Mo's flat. Mo said she wanted something smaller and Marjorie found her a decent-sized room with a small kitchen, quite nearby. Mo listened to Marjorie's plans for working in the school in Camden Town without comment. Marjorie explained that it would keep her busy, and she would be close if Mo needed her. Mo seemed uninterested in the plans and asked no questions. She merely shrugged, seeming to say that what people did was their own concern, nothing to do with her.

Marjorie finished her tea and gave Tina the empty cup to take in. It was nearly time for the whistle. She looked around the playground, and watched the children shouting and running with increased intensity as they sensed the imminent end of playtime. She knew them all now, fifty small children with an extraordinary variety of lives. They all put what they knew of life into practice in the playground; the ones like Tina who stood outside, or were accepted into a group only on suffrance or a temporary basis. You could see, as they played, the anxiety in their eyes: how long would this last? The fear of being told to go away spoiling the pleasure of being for the present part of it all. Others, quite different, organizing, being called on to decide what was to be played, who was in or out, shouldering their responsibilities lightly, expecting deference. And the rest, shifting positions, deciding to settle for one of the less powerful groupings because they had more chance of acceptance and a better position.

Marjorie could chart the pain and pleasure of these small children learning to be adults. She watched them and knew there was nothing she should do other than be there, an adult presence that kept the life and death games within limits. She listened but did not interfere unless something had gone too far. Her involvement with the children was bounded by the walls of the playground. Outside there was nothing she could do about their difficulties and sorrows, but within the walls she was there, concerned and caring, listening to what they had to tell her, looking at the special things they brought in to show her. It was a small, definite role. A practical involvement.

The infants liked Mrs Singleton. They liked her kind, blue eyes and her soft, wavy, fading blonde hair. For some of them, she would be one of a series of moments of their childhood. They would look back and remember her standing by the playground wall chatting and smiling and listening to them. For a few, Tina perhaps, she would be the single good memory they retained of their early days at school. Warm, comfortable and safe. The person who was there when they couldn't sort things out for themselves and needed an understanding grown-up to mediate.

Marjorie thought, as she blew the whistle to signal the end of playtime, that really she had been fortunate.

Seventeen

It's been several weeks now since I had a dream. I have been enjoying restful nights and I'm beginning to believe that I have really put all that behind me.

The last dream I had was hardly a forest dream at all. It was there, grey-green and misty in the background, but not dominating and threatening like the others. Just a pale, disappearing backdrop. I had been – I don't know – asleep. More like unconscious. And as the dream began I was coming round. I say 'me', because it felt like me, but as I rose to awareness I had no recollection of who I was at all. No past, no history. I came awake as if I had just been born, and although there was no memory of it, I knew for certain that I had lived a life.

There were figures, several of them, at the foot of my bed; very tall and thin. Wraithlike, covered from head to foot in robes made of coarse grey stuff, like habits. Their faces were concealed by the draping hoods that hung down below their foreheads. Perhaps they had no faces at all. They stood there, maybe half a dozen of them, in silence, but a silence so profound it seemed that they created it and put it out into the world. Silence exuded from them, and they stood there, completely still, as if they had been there for aeons, waiting. I knew they had. That they had been waiting for me to come round, but with no sense of urgency. They had stood, for who knows how long, and would have continued to stand for as long as necessary.

I understood this immediately, and the fact that I was in some way in their charge, their care. Their eternal patience was their caring: there was no warmth, nothing that could be simply defined as friendliness; just the acceptance and the waiting. All this was clear to me as I opened my eyes, but still I had no notion of who or what I was. Nor was there much curiosity on my part. I accepted their presence without wanting to ask questions.

As I said, the forest was hardly there, just a shadow in the background. It seemed that the walls of the room were made of forest, but still were walls. There was nothing disturbing, and I lay in the room gathering my strength.

Later they came in with a child. One of the long grey figures held it, an infant, against his chest, swathed in material, a kind of shawl made of the same stuff as their robes. I understood that this was my child, that I had borne it, although I had no recollection of its existence at all. And this was why they waited. It seemed they were taking care of it until I was able to take over. But there was no sense of hurry, and I was too weak to do more than look at the small bundle at the other side of the room.

Time passed, and my task was to get stronger. I got up and began to walk the featureless corridors outside my room. Gradually I felt strength building in me, a kind of solidity that grew up through my spine and seemed to make the world outside less misty, more solid itself. And then I had the child. I walked along the corridor and held the baby encased in its shawl against me. It was warm and quiet, and there was a peaceful pleasure in holding it and pacing gently, regularly up and down. But suddenly I realized that there was no baby inside the shawl, that I clutched only empty material against me. I turned, terrified, not knowing how long it was since I had lost the child. It had slipped over my shoulder, and I hadn't noticed. It seemed then that everything was lost. That I was lost in this grey place where there was nothing, where I was nothing.

I was appalled and ashamed at my failure, my neglect.

Then I turned and saw the hooded figures behind me. They had the child. They had been following me all along and caught it before it fell, then walked behind me in their silence, for how long I have no idea, waiting for me to notice the absence. There was no judgement at all, no blame. They would go on watching and waiting for as long as it took me to become fully myself; fully aware for long enough to take the child and look after it without their assistance. In the meantime they remained, strong and caring. Distant, but always there.

When I woke I couldn't make it out at all. The atmosphere of the dream stayed with me for days, like the grey mist of the dream itself. It was strange, the combination of coldness and concern, and the sense I had that I would only become solid myself if I took the child on. It meant nothing to me, but wouldn't quite go away. But then I remembered how vague the forest had been. If the forest was going away then I was getting better, I decided.

I told Dr Taylor the following week that I didn't think I needed to see him any more. He suggested I stay a little longer, but I insisted, and in the weeks since there have been no more dreams. No forests, no guardians. And I wake well rested, ready for the day's schedule.

Everything is going well.

I visit Nick once a week at the hospital. He's much calmer now, although sometimes there's a remote look in his eyes as if he were listening to something that I can't hear. But he talks and behaves normally. He's agreed to give up The Book for the time being, and the psychiatric social worker is trying to sort out something for him to do when he leaves. I suppose the truth is that he will have to be stabilized on drugs permanently, but that isn't so deadful compared to the pain I saw him in when he was at his worst.

And I see Marjorie, of course. Now that she's in London three days a week I see her more often. Usually she comes here for tea on Wednesday after she finishes at the school. It seems to be good for her. I suppose she must have been getting bored alone in the country for so long. That's understandable. This job gives her a change of scenery and a chance to get out and meet people. It gives her an interest. If that's what she wants I'm pleased for her. It's nice to see her managing better. She seems to get on well with the children and tells me about them when she comes round. I listen.

I don't regret the flat at all. It was a good idea having Marjorie take it over. There was too much of it. The carpet and furniture, all the shelves and books. The things. When I thought of going back to it, in the hospital, it seemed terribly cluttered. It'll suit Marjorie better.

It does seem to me that things have worked out. I don't miss the university at all. Occasionally I get a card from Liam in Lusaka, but I haven't got round to writing back. He came to see me at the hospital, but I didn't feel very much like talking. There are some relationships that end once a distance has been placed between them. It wasn't more than a working friendship.

Joe, I understand, is living in Sydney.

I don't remember now why I got into such a state. Too many things happened at once, none of them, in retrospect, of any real importance, but happening together as they did making it seem as if they mattered. As if something serious was happening. As I say, I know now they weren't actually serious, just a distortion of my vision. Things are back in focus now.

I've been thinking of taking on a couple more houses. I have enough time, and several people have mentioned that they would like me to work for them. I'll go and see them next week and decide then. But I don't want to take on too much. I want time to spend here, peacefully, in my own space.

This room is quite perfect. When Marjorie found it for me, she furnished it, ready for me to move into when I left the hospital. Once I got here, it was necessary to get rid of a great deal.

The flooring was fine, plain wooden boards, no carpet, and just a couple of rugs Marjorie had put down that were easy to dispose of. And the white walls needed nothing once I'd taken down the two little landscapes that she had brought from the house in Sussex. In this room I have a bed and a chair, and by one wall a small wooden table where I eat and sit to write these notes. That's all, apart from a few books stacked vertically in one corner. I'm not sure I really need the armchair. There's the bed to sit and lie on, and the wooden chair at the table. I may get rid of it. It's not necessary and takes up space.

My room, here, where I live, is a place I hardly have to notice at all. An almost empty space that requires nothing of me. Occasionally

I sweep the floorboards and wipe the top of the table, but it makes very little difference. I live, contented, in an environment to which I am indifferent. My days are spent in making other people's environments right for them, that is my work. But this is where I live.

I like it, my space. An empty space. Tidy and empty.

FOR THE BEST IN PAPERBACKS, LOOK FOR THE

In every corner of the world, on every subject under the sun, Penguin represents quality and variety – the very best in publishing today.

For complete information about books available from Penguin – including Puffins, Penguin Classics and Arkana – and how to order them, write to us at the appropriate address below. Please note that for copyright reasons the selection of books varies from country to country.

In the United Kingdom: Please write to *Dept E.P., Penguin Books Ltd, Harmondsworth, Middlesex, UB7 0DA*.

If you have any difficulty in obtaining a title, please send your order with the correct money, plus ten per cent for postage and packaging, to *PO Box No 11, West Drayton, Middlesex*

In the United States: Please write to *Dept BA, Penguin, 299 Murray Hill Parkway, East Rutherford, New Jersey 07073*

In Canada: Please write to *Penguin Books Canada Ltd, 2801 John Street, Markham, Ontario L3R 1B4*

In Australia: Please write to the *Marketing Department, Penguin Books Australia Ltd, P.O. Box 257, Ringwood, Victoria 3134*

In New Zealand: Please write to the *Marketing Department, Penguin Books (NZ) Ltd, Private Bag, Takapuna, Auckland 9*

In India: Please write to *Penguin Overseas Ltd, 706 Eros Apartments, 56 Nehru Place, New Delhi, 110019*

In the Netherlands: Please write to *Penguin Books Netherlands B.V., Postbus 195, NL–1380AD Weesp*

In West Germany: Please write to *Penguin Books Ltd, Friedrichstrasse 10–12, D–6000 Frankfurt/Main 1*

In Spain: Please write to *Alhambra Longman S.A., Fernandez de la Hoz 9, E–28010 Madrid*

In Italy: Please write to *Penguin Italia s.r.l., Via Como 4, I-20096 Pioltello (Milano)*

In France: Please write to *Penguin Books Ltd, 39 Rue de Montmorency, F-75003 Paris*

In Japan: Please write to *Longman Penguin Japan Co Ltd, Yamaguchi Building, 2–12–9 Kanda Jimbocho, Chiyoda-Ku, Tokyo 101*